DAILY READINGS WITH
WILLIAM BARCLAY

Books by William Barclay
available as Fount Paperbacks

Ethics in a Permissive Society
More Prayers for the Plain Man
More Prayers for Young People
The Plain Man Looks at the Apostles' Creed
The Plain Man Looks at the Beatitudes
The Plain Man's Book of Prayers
The Plain Man's Guide to Ethics
Prayers for Help and Healing
Prayers for Young People

Edited by Rita Snowden

In the Hands of God

DAILY READINGS WITH
WILLIAM BARCLAY

Edited by
RONALD BARCLAY

Fount
An Imprint of HarperCollins*Publishers*

Fount Paperbacks
is an Imprint of HarperCollins*Religious*
Part of HarperCollins*Publishers*
77–85 Fulham Palace Road,
Hammersmith, London W6 8JB

Published by Fount Paperbacks 1991
1 3 5 7 9 10 8 6 4 2

A catalogue record for this book
is available from the British Library

ISBN 0 00 627518 4

Printed in Great Britain by
HarperCollinsManufacturing Glasgow

CONTENTS

INTRODUCTION

My father, William Barclay, was born in Wick in Caithness in North Scotland on 5th December 1907. His father was forty-one and his mother thirty-eight, and he was an only child. His father was a bank teller who later became a bank manager, and from his early years Willie was accustomed to having well respected parents. His theology was created in a happy, privileged home where he experienced the security of growing up under the care of two intelligent and contented people. "Whatever I have done in life," he said, "it is because I stood on the shoulders of my parents."

My grandfather belonged to the evangelical wing of the Church, and my father was brought up in a home of strictly conservative theological belief. Despite later criticisms of being "too liberal" it is true to say that he never stopped believing that his main aim in life was to win souls for Christ.

When my father was five, my grandfather was promoted to Motherwell, a town in central Scotland. In 1913 the young Willie became seriously ill after an attack of scarlet fever which left his hearing severely impaired. It is strange that one of Scotland's greatest communicators of the spoken and written word had great difficulty in hearing from an early age. Some of my earliest memories of my father are of him escaping from the bustle of everyday life, simply by turning down the volume on his hearing aid and retreating into a world of peace and quiet! Typically, he used what could have been an impossible disability to his advantage.

He attended Dalziel High School in Motherwell, and his record in the classroom and on the sportsfield was one of unqualified success. In the summer of 1920 he resolved to become a minister. He used to talk about the stone in the road in Fort William, a town in the north of Scotland, where he made his decision while on holiday there. In October 1925 he went to Glasgow University, and graduated in 1929 with a First Class Honours degree in Latin and Greek. In 1932 he was awarded a BD with distinction, and the path was set for a long and distinguished career.

Tragedy struck shortly before he was to be licensed to become a minister of the Church of Scotland. His mother died of cancer of the spine. "You'll have a new note in your preaching now", my grandfather said to him. My father dedicated his first important book, *Daily Study Bible Readings from Acts* to his parents: "In grateful memory of W.D.B. and B.L.B. from whose lips I first heard the name of Jesus and in whose lives I first saw Him."

Before embarking on his career, my father spent a semester at the University of Marburg in Germany and studied under Professor Bultmann. Bultmann argued for a modern approach to traditional beliefs and instilled in my father the desire to explore in detail the background to Jesus and the New Testament, a stimulus which stayed with him throughout his academic life.

On 9th January 1933 he preached as sole nominee for Trinity Church, Renfrew on the Clydeside, a church which had never managed to keep a minister for more than four years. It was, indeed, a baptism of fire! My father loved to tell the story of how one evening, when he had returned home after a particularly vigorous church meeting and was recounting how he had been drained by the arguments and very lively discussion, the telephone rang and the voice at the other end of the line said, "That was a great argument we had tonight, Mr Barclay!" (My father's entry in *Who's Who* under hobbies ran, "Music and arguments"!)

He certainly learned how to communicate with people in

8

those days in Renfrew. For fourteen years he ministered to Trinity Church, and much of his later success comes from what he learned from his congregation. He used to put his ability to communicate down to the wisdom of one old lady who had been confined to her house by illness. When my father visited her, he sat down on the edge of the bed and began to speak to her. After a few moments she interrupted him, ''Mr Barclay, when you talk to me like this I can understand every word you say, but when you're in the pulpit on Sunday, I don't know what you are going on about!'' He never forgot that, and he aimed to communicate with people as though he was sitting beside them, talking just to them and to no one else.

My father married my mother on 30th June 1933, and since she was one of five sisters and my grandmother had a very dominant and forceful personality, my poor father sometimes struggled to get a word in edgeways until I appeared on the scene on 29 September 1934 to give him some male support! He sometimes quoted this poem, no doubt to relieve his feelings:

> Lord on whom all love depends
> Let us make and keep good friends.
> Bless me also with the patience
> To endure my wife's relations!

It is interesting to note that my father was very much a man's man and often happier in male company. A whole series of his books is entitled *The Plain Man looks at . . .* and I do not think that he chose that title by pure chance.

My sister, Barbara, was born in June 1937 and the family circle was complete.

They were happy days in Renfrew. The membership of the church and the Sunday School rose steadily. My father's first attempts at writing were for Sunday School teachers, and in his time he wrote two hundred and thirty-seven lessons, and also became Convenor of the Youth Committee of the Church of Scotland. Then, to my consternation, since I did not want to move, my father announced his resignation in October 1946, and on 1st January 1947 he began a career as lecturer in New Testament Language and Literature at Glasgow University, the start of an era which was to make his name known in almost every household in the land.

Not content just to concentrate on his lectures, my father continued to write for the *Scottish Sunday School Teacher* magazine. He produced syllabuses for day school teachers. For thirty years he wrote a column for the *Expository Times*, and he wrote a page for ministers in the *British Weekly*. Conferences, meetings, discussions with Army Chaplains at Bagshot, Immortal Memories at Burns Suppers, a never-ending round of engagements filled his life and he thrived on it all. Despite this constant activity my father always had time for the family, and I still have vivid memories, not only of happy holidays spent as a child with my parents and my sister, but also of holidays where my wife and I, along with our three children, accompanied my father and mother on joint holidays to Elie, a small seaside town on the east coast of Scotland.

A remarkable feature of my father's life and works was that he was acceptable to a very large section of the community. The Salvation Army, the Roman Catholic Church, the academic world, ministers of all denominations, ordinary people from every walk of life found in his talks and his writings something which appealed to them. He became a guide and mentor to countless people. One of his first books, *Ambassador for Christ: the life and teaching of St Paul*, was originally written for Junior Bible Classes, and he included in his writings at this time handbooks for the Boys' Brigade. Between 1950 and 1981, in twenty-two of the thirty-two annual sessions, my father's books were used to help the

Boys' Brigade movement. Professor George Knight of New Zealand wrote, "William Barclay always expounded the New Testament as if he were addressing his senior Bible Class." My father's aim was indeed to make the New Testament accessible to all, and it is surely for this that he will be remembered.

My father's most important achievement is considered by many to be the *Daily Bible Study Readings*, now called the *Daily Study Bible*, a commentary on all the books of the New Testament. The irony is that he was a stop-gap to help the Church of Scotland in a moment of crisis when a publication was suddenly needed! Some ten million copies later we can only wonder at the incredible way it all started. There are German, Norwegian, Indonesian and Russian translations of the D.S.B., as it is known, and other books have been translated into Chinese, Japanese, Spanish, French, Afrikaans, etc. Countless people have been helped by my father's aim "to make the life and words of Jesus live". He was not a systematic theologian, and his claim to fame rests on his use of biblical material to interpret, illustrate and expand the text.

The *Daily Bible Study Readings* were completed on his fifty-first birthday in December 1958. On 6th July 1956 the degree of DD was conferred on him by Edinburgh University, a wonderful moment of recognition of all that he had done to bring the life and words of Jesus, not only to the man and woman in the pew, but also to the "unchurched masses", as he put it.

Then the suffering and pain which never left him struck again. My sister, Barbara, aged nineteen, was drowned in a tragic boating accident in Northern Ireland on 10th August of the same year. "This is only the end of one chapter," he said, "it is not the end of the book." The agony for him and my mother was unbearable.

When my father died on 24th January 1978 we found a

letter in his jacket pocket. We knew about the letter, but we did not know that he had kept it. The letter said:

> Dear Dr Barclay,
> I know why God killed your daughter. It was to save her from being corrupted by your heresies.
> signed:
> A Christian.

My father's very open and sometimes incautious approach left him open to much criticism, but he did not deserve such a heartless comment.

In 1957 my mother and father adopted my sister, Jane, then aged five, and the happiness she brought to them helped to restore the family circle, and laughter and fun returned to our house again.

By March 1960 he had published thirty-three books and he used to delight in calling himself ''a theological middle man''. In 1962 he started a series of television broadcasts which enthralled a nation. Few people would willingly have missed the William Barclay Lectures on television on a Sunday evening. His West of Scotland accent, his very rapid delivery, and his habit of pacing up and down should have made his television appearances a disaster, but the force of his personality and the power of his faith shone through. Ironically, he had been successful in radio broadcasts but had been very reluctant to move into television, perhaps fearing that he could not submit himself to its constraints. In the end television submitted to him!

In 1963, at the age of fifty-six, he was appointed Professor to the Chair of Divinity and Biblical Criticism at the University of Glasgow, and he remained in that post until he retired in 1974. The time taken to make the appointment was inordinately long, no doubt on account of doubts about his scholarship; but he suffered as a result. Despite his strong personality and granite-like outward appearance my father was a sensitive, vulnerable person who disliked fuss and publicity. He was happiest with the family and his beloved Staffordshire Bull Terrier, Rusty, or sitting in his car at the seaside or in the country, reading and snoozing. He was, however, an incurable and unrepentant optimist, and I am convinced that he was often surprised by the controversy he raised, and that a certain naïveté caused many of the problems he encountered throughout his life.

The controversy reached a climax in 1967 when he turned down the nomination to be Moderator of the General Assembly of the Church of Scotland, the highest honour for a minister of that denomination. He did not want to interrupt his ministry to his students or to "the plain man". "I felt I was totally unfitted to that kind of duty. I have never been a member of the Establishment. It's not for me."

In 1967 his translation of the New Testament appeared, and in 1969 he gave his penultimate television series. The strain had begun to tell, and my father became seriously ill in 1969. His habit of smoking far too many cigarettes a day had destroyed his lungs and he had emphysema. Far worse, he was told he had Parkinson's Disease and that he had eight years to live. The suffering which was never far from his life would not let him go. I can well remember counting the years, the months, the weeks, the days. And the doctors were right. He died eight years later, just as they had diagnosed.

In September 1974 he retired from his Chair, and the very next day he took a room in Collins' offices in Glasgow to continue his work, this time preparing a commentary on the Old Testament. He only managed to complete a few chapters on the Psalms, and the book was published after his death under the title *The Lord is my Shepherd*. Even in the last shadowy days my father never lost his faith or the trust he had in the Jesus who can heal all our pains.

I well remember the end coming just after Christmas in 1977. Our elder daughter was saying goodbye to her grandfather before going back to France to continue with her au-pair job there, and the tears in my father's eyes told me that he knew he would not see her again.

William Barclay shines through the pages of this book. He was a wonderful husband, father and grandfather, but above all, he was Christ's man. "The others we know about, Jesus we know. The others we remember, Jesus we experience", he loved to say, and his whole aim in life he summed up in Richard of Chichester's prayer: "to know Jesus Christ more clearly, to love him more dearly and to follow him more nearly." His favourite words came from Isaac Watts' hymn, words which he sang with his beloved Trinity College Choir at every concert they gave:

> Were the whole realm of nature mine,
> That were an offering far too small;
> Love so amazing, so divine,
> Demands my soul, my life, my all.

THE SEEKING GOD

God, as the Christian knows him, is the *seeking* God. The great liberal Jewish scholar C. G. Montefiore held strongly that this is the one absolutely new thing which Jesus came to say. The idea of a God who will *invite* the sinner back is not new; the idea of a God who will *welcome* back the penitent sinner is not new; but the idea of a God who will go and seek for the sinner, and who wants men to do the same, is something completely new. Montefiore would find the very centre and soul and essence of the Christian Gospel in Luke 15:1–10, in the story of the shepherd searching for the lost sheep and the woman searching for the lost coin. He writes: "Jesus sought to bring back into glad communion with God those whom sin, whether 'moral' or 'ceremonial', had driven away. For him sinners (at least certain types of sinners) were the subject not of condemnation or disdain, but of pity. He did not avoid sinners, he sought them out. They were still children of God. This was a new and sublime contribution to the development of religion and morality . . . To deny the greatness and originality of Jesus in this connection, to deny that he opened a new chapter in men's attitude to sin and sinners is, I think, to beat the head against the wall." "The virtues of repentance are gloriously praised in the Rabbinical literature, but this direct search for, and appeal to, the sinner are new and moving notes of high import and significance."

It is not so very difficult to think of a God who will forgive the sinner who comes humbly and penitently back to him on his hands and knees; but no man outside Christianity had ever thought of a God who would deliberately go out and seek for the sinner until he found him and brought him home.

All this goes to show that in Christianity there is

established a quite new relationship between God and man. The relationships of king and subject, master and slave, judge and criminal, immortal and mortal, holy one and sinner, are all obvious and natural. All these relationships are in one way or another based on a relationship whose essence is law. The idea is that God lays down his law; man obeys or disobeys, accepts or rejects; and is accordingly found innocent or guilty. What Christianity does is to remove the fear and the distance in the relationship between man and God, and establish first and foremost a relationship of love, the relationship of father and son.

The Plain Man Looks at the Apostles' Creed, pp. 47–48

O God,
I have no one of my own at all now,
There isn't anyone to think about me
  or to worry about me.
I have friends and acquaintances,
  but I have no one at home
  of my own flesh and blood.
I'm not worried about being looked after.
I know that that will be done all right.
  But I can't help feeling lonely,
  and I can't help envying others
  who have people who really care for them.
Help me to remember that
  I have you as my Father,
And that I have Jesus
  as the Brother born to help
  in time of trouble.
And so help me to lose my loneliness
  in your love.

I can say with the Psalmist:
    Whom have I in heaven but thee?
    And there is nothing upon earth that
    I desire beside thee.   *Psalm 73:25*

I've found a friend; O such a friend!
    He loved me ere I knew him;
He drew me with the cords of love,
    And thus he bound me to him;
And round my heart still closely twine
    These ties which nought can sever,
For I am his, and he is mine,
    For ever and for ever.

                    Prayers for Help and Healing, p. 37

WHAT GOD IS LIKE

Before Jesus came no man knew what God was like; men thought of God as king and judge, as justice and holiness, as wrath and vengeance; but they never conceived of the supreme wonder of the love of God. So in Jesus Christ God comes to men, and he says: "I love you like that." When we see Jesus healing the sick, feeding the hungry, being the friend of outcasts and sinners, this is God saying: "I love you like that." When we see Jesus still refusing to do anything but love, even when men betray and insult and revile him, this is God saying: "I love you like that." And, if Jesus had stopped before the cross, it would have meant that there was some point beyond which the love of God would not go, but because Jesus, having loved men, loved them to the end, it means that there is nothing which can

17

alter the love of God. It means that God in Jesus Christ says: "You can betray me; you can hate me; you can misjudge me; you can scourge me; you can crucify me; and nothing you can do can alter my love." No man ever thought of God like that and no man ever could have thought of God like that. This is staggeringly new and utterly undiscoverable by any human means. Only Jesus Christ could tell men that. And therefore it is most literally true to say that *it cost the life and death of Jesus Christ to reconcile men to God*. Had it not been for the life and the death and the cross of Christ, no man would ever have known what God is like.

And so the essence of Jesus is not that he altered God, not that he changed a wrathful and offended God into a loving and forgiving God, but that he died to show men what God is always like, not that he should threaten us into a prudential response, but that at the sight of him we should be moved and compelled to love him as he first loved us. Jesus came not to persuade God to forgive us, but to tell us that God in his love has forgiven us, and that all that we can do is in wondering gratitude to accept the forgiveness of sins, which it cost the cross to make known to us.

The Plain Man Looks at the Apostles' Creed, pp. 331–32

O God, help me to think all through today in every word and in every action and in every situation of what Jesus would do.

Help me to think of how Jesus went to school and learned and grew in wisdom, just as I must do.

Help me to think how he worked in the carpenter's shop and learned a trade, just as I must do.

Help me to remember how he obeyed his parents, just as I must do.

Help me to remember how he found people unjust and

unfair and unsympathetic and unkind, just as may happen to me.

Help me to remember how his friends let him down, just as may happen to me.

Help me to remember that he loved us all so much that he gave for us everything he had, even his life, just as I ought to do.

He has left us an example that we should follow in his steps. Help me to follow in his steps all through today.

This I ask for your love's sake. Amen.

Prayers for Young People, p. 70

THERE IS NO ONE GOD DOES NOT KNOW BY NAME

Paul Tournier, the great Christian doctor, tells a tragic thing. In *A Doctor's Casebook* he writes: ''There was one patient of mine, the youngest daughter in a large family, which the father found it difficult to support. One day she heard him mutter despairingly, referring to herself: 'We could well have done without that one!' '' That is precisely what God can never say. In the same book Paul Tournier notes another thing. God says to Moses: ''I know thee *by name*'' (Exodus 33:17). He says to Cyrus: ''I am the Lord, which call thee *by thy name*'' (Isaiah 45:3). One of the features of the Bible is whole chapters of names, of genealogies. There was a time when Paul Tournier thought that these chapters could well have been omitted from the Bible, and then he came to see that they are the symbol of the infinite number of people whom God knows *by name*. The love of God is so detailed that the worthless sparrow matters to him, that there is no

19

one whom he does not know by name. In point of fact the saying about the sparrow may be even more wonderful yet. "Not one of them will fall to the ground without your Father's will." We might think that that refers to the *death* of a sparrow. But my old teacher J. E. McFadyen used to love to suggest that, if we put that saying back into Aramaic, it may well mean, not that God sees it if a sparrow *falls* to the ground, but if a sparrow *lights* on the ground. Every time the sparrow hops on the ground God sees it and knows.

Every time we pray, "Our Father", we can know for certain that for God no one is lost in the crowd; that if we matter to no one else, we matter to God; that if no one else cares for us, God cares. Here is something to lift up our hearts every time we pray our Lord's prayer.

The Plain Man looks at the Lord's Prayer, p. 44

O God, bless all my friends and my loved ones tonight:

Bless those whose lives are interwoven with mine, and without whom life could never be the same. Bless those to whom I owe my comfort, and without whom life would be very lonely.

Bless the one to whom I have given my heart to keep, and who has given me his/her heart to keep, and keep us for ever loyal, for ever loving, and for ever true to one another.

Bless my absent friends and loved ones, from whom for a time I am separated. Guard them, guide them, protect them, and grant that we may soon meet again.

I know that all for whom I am praying are also praying for me. Help me just now to feel very near to them, and not only to them, but even to those whom I have loved and lost awhile, and who have gone to be with you.

Hear this my prayer for your love's sake. Amen.

More Prayers for the Plain Man, pp. 64–65

"OH, HOW I LOVE THY LAW!"

Thomas Carlyle could say the bluntest things. He was told of a lavender-and-lace type of gushing lady who remarked that she accepted the world. "By God," commented Carlyle, "she'd better!"

This is indeed acceptance of the will of God, but it is completely joyless; it is tired and weary and defeated and resigned, not content, still less glad, but only resigned to the fact that things must be so. There are many who live in a grey acceptance that things are as they are.

It can be spoken in the tone of voice of one who *in the end accepts something, not exactly in weary resignation, but in the conviction that he cannot in any event do anything about it,* the tone of voice of one who yields with a more or less good grace to *force majeure.* In *Courage to Change,* her study of Reinhold Niebuhr, June Bingham tells a story which Niebuhr loved to tell. Reinhold Niebuhr wanted his daughter to come out for a walk, and she did not want to go. He extolled the virtues of exercise and fresh air, and in the end she came. As they ended their walk, he turned to her and said: "Now aren't you glad that you decided to come?" Whereat his daughter replied: "I didn't decide. You were just bigger!" Her philosophy was that it was better to do without a struggle what in the end you would be

21

compelled to do anyway! There are some people who accept the will of God just because God is ''bigger''. They are not particularly resentful; and they are not particularly defeated and resigned; but equally they have no thrill and throb of joy in making God's will their choice. They could never say: ''Oh, how I *love* thy law!''

The Plain Man Looks at the Lord's Prayer, pp. 80–81

O God,
Sometimes I lie here and worry.
I worry
  about what is going to happen to myself,
  about what is going to happen to my work and to my job,
  and to those who are depending on me.
I worry
  about what is going to happen to the house and home,
  and about what is happening to the family
  with me not there.
After all, it would hardly be natural
  if I didn't.
I fear the worst,
  and sometimes I wonder
  if I am ever going to be well and strong again.
Give me
  the peace of mind
  which comes
  from leaving things to you.
Help me
  to feel the clasp of the everlasting arms
  underneath and about me,
  and to know
  that neither I nor those I love
  can ever drift
  beyond your love and care.

Let me remember the promise of Jesus:
  Peace I leave with you; my peace I give to you;
  not as the world gives do I give to you. Let not
  your hearts be troubled, neither let them be afraid.

John 14:27

I know not what the future hath
Of marvel or surprise,
Assured alone that life and death
His mercy underlies.

Prayers for Help and Healing, p. 31

"IT IS GOD'S WILL"

Nothing has done the Christian faith and the Church more
harm than the indiscriminate and blasphemous use of the
phrase, "It is God's will". There are people who will go
into a home in which a child has been killed in a street
accident, in which a young life has been cut off before
it has ever had time to blossom, in which a man or a
woman is suffering agonies from some disease that not
all the skill of man can help, in which untimely death
has reft a mother from her children or a father from the
family which was dependent on him, and who will say,
"It is God's will". There are those who will hear of a
terrible accident on the road, at sea, or in the air, or from
some cataclysm in nature and who will say, "It is God's
will". Such things are not the will of God. It is not God's
will ever that a child should be needlessly killed by some
reckless or drunken fool in a motor car, or that someone
should be agonised by some disease which is the enemy

23

of life. This is the direct opposite of the will of God; *this is the result of the sin of man,* not necessarily the sin of the sufferer, but the sin of the human situation of which the sufferer is a part. It is precisely such pain and sorrow and suffering that Jesus came to defeat, as his healing and miraculous powers show. It is a blasphemous slander on God to attribute to him acts and situations and events which, if we believe in the love of God in Jesus Christ, are the exact opposite of his will.

It may be the will of God – it often is – that we have to take some heart-breaking decision, that we have to accept some poignant disappointment, that we have to make some agonizing sacrifice, that we have to face some way from which our whole being shrinks. It is at such a moment as that, that we must be quite sure of the wise and loving will of God, no matter what it feels like.

But in these moments of human sin and agony and human sorrow, what *do* we say? We have to say: "This is not God's will. This is the result in some way of the sin and the folly of man. You have been bitterly involved in this. God did not send it to you. But God can bring you through it, still erect, still steady-eyed, and still on your own two feet. And more, much more, out of this bitter thing you can come stronger, and purer, and nearer God and better able to help men, than ever you were before. For God can work for good even things that are outside his will, to those who trust and love him." We can say: "If you will allow God to use this and to use you, this, even this, can *become* part of his will."

My mother died of cancer of the spine in such a way and out of such a pain that it was a relief to see her release. She was a saint, and the sorrow was very sore. But I can remember my father coming to me to this day and saying to me: "You will have a new note in your preaching now." And it was so, in the goodness of God, because I was better able to

24

help others who were going through it, because I had gone through it.

The Plain Man Looks at the Lord's Prayer, pp. 84–86

O God,
Help me to say:
  Your will be done.
Help me
  to be quite sure
    that all things do work together for good.
Help me to remember and to discover
  that even pain and weakness
    can bring me nearer you,
  and that the dews of sorrow
    can be lustred by your love.
Help me to remember
  that it is your promise,
    that neither I nor anyone else
  will be tested above what we can bear.
Help me to remember
  that a father's hand will never cause
    his child a needless tear.
Help me
  to say, as my Blessed Lord said,
    "Into your hands I commit my spirit".

Let me remember Jesus' last prayer:
  Father, into your hands I commit my spirit. *Luke 23:46*

Not mine, not mine the choice,
  In things or great or small;
Be thou my guide and strength,
  My wisdom and my all.

Prayers for Help and Healing, p. 51

SOMEWHERE THERE MUST BE A WORLD-MAKER

There is what is perhaps the most famous of all arguments, the argument from design. This is an argument for the existence of God which men have used for thousands of years. A modern example of it is the parable of Paley. Suppose a man is walking across a moor and he happens to hit his foot against a watch. He picks it up; he has never seen a watch before; he examines it. He sees that the hands are moving round the dial in what is clearly an orderly way. He opens it up and he finds inside a host of wheels and cogs and levers and springs and jewels. He discovers that by winding up the watch, you can set it going, and that the whole complicated machinery is moving in what is obviously a predetermined pattern. What then does he say? Does he say: "By chance all these wheels and levers and jewels and springs came together and formed themselves into this thing I have in my hand. By chance they set themselves going. By chance they move in an orderly way. By chance this watch became an instrument which counts the hours and minutes and seconds"? No. If he applies his mind to this problem at all, he says: "I have found a watch. *Somewhere there must be a watchmaker.*" So then when we discover a world where there is an order more accurate than any watch, where tides ebb and flow according to schedule, where spring, summer, autumn and winter come back in unvarying succession, where the planets never leave their courses, where the same cause always produces the same effect, we are bound to say: "I have found a world. *Somewhere there must be a world-maker.*"

The Plain Man Looks at the Apostles' Creed, p. 28

O God, my Father, thank you for the world in which I live.
Thank you
    For all the beautiful things in it;
    For all the interesting things in it;
    For all the useful things in it.
Thank you for the life which you have given me.
Thank you for
    My body to act;
    My mind to think;
    My memory to remember;
    My heart to love.
Thank you for giving me
    So many things to enjoy;
    So many things to learn;
    So many things to do;
    So many people to love.
Help me never to do anything which would make the world
uglier or people sadder. Help me always to add something
to the world's beauty and to the world's joy: through Jesus
Christ my Lord. Amen.

Prayers for Young People, p. 86

TIME, AS GOD SEES IT

The more we know of the universe the more staggering its
sheer immensity becomes. Hendrik van Loon in his book,
The Home of Mankind, presents us with certain figures about
the world in which we live. Astronomers speak about stars
and planets being so many "light years" away. Light travels
at the rate of 186,000 miles per second. That is to say, in
one year lights travels $186,000 \times 60 \times 60 \times 24 \times 365$ miles. So

when an astronomer speaks of a star or a planet as being so many light years away, he means that the light from that planet has taken that number of years to reach us, travelling all the time at 186,000 miles per second. The light from Alpha Centauri, the nearest star to this earth, takes 4 years 3 months to reach us. The light from the Pole Star takes 466 years to reach us. That is to say, the Pole Star is $186,000 \times 60 \times 60 \times 24 \times 365 \times 466$ miles away from this earth.

Such figures are frankly inconceivable for the ordinary mind. So Hendrik van Loon has expressed it in a different way. He has expressed it in the time that it would take an express train travelling day and night to reach certain stars and planets. It would need 300 years to get to the sun; it would take 8,300 years to reach Neptune; it would take 75,000,000 to reach Alpha Centauri, the nearest star; and it would take 700,000,000 years to reach the Pole Star. Ten million generations of men would have lived and died before that celestial train got there. This is to say that the light we see from the Pole Star left that star in AD 1596, fifteen years before the Authorized Version of the Bible was made, and has been travelling towards this earth at the rate of 186,000 miles per second ever since.

When we think of figures like that, we can catch some faint glimpse of the sheer majestic and infinite power of the divine mind which created, orders and sustains all that.

Or let us think of this in terms of time. Suppose we take the whole length of Cleopatra's needle, and suppose on the top of it we stick one single postage stamp, the thickness of the postage stamp would represent the time during which man as man has been in being, and the length of the whole monument would represent the probable length of time the world existed before man came into it at all. Human history represents the merest fraction of time.

Time like that leaves the human mind baffled and amazed, and yet that is time as God sees it.

The Plain Man Looks at the Apostles' Creed, pp. 34–35

O God, my Father, as I go out to life and work today,

I thank you for the world's beauty:
  For the light of the sun;
  For the wind on my face;
  For the colour of the flowers;
  And for all glimpses of lovely things.

I thank you for life's gracious things:
  For friendship's help;
  For kinship's strength;
  For love's wonder.

I remember this world's evil and its sin.
  Help me to overcome every temptation, and make my life like a light which guides to goodness. And, if anyone has fallen, help me to sympathize and to help rather than to judge and condemn.

I remember this world's sorrow.
  Help me today to bring comfort to some broken heart, and cheer to some lonely life.

So grant that, when evening comes, I may feel that I have not wasted this day.

Hear this my prayer through Jesus Christ my Lord. Amen.

More Prayers for the Plain Man, p. 46

ABSOLUTE LOVE

It is told that once in the days before the ending of slavery, Lincoln bought a slave girl with the sole purpose of giving her her freedom. She did not realize why he was buying her; she thought that it was simply another transaction in which she was involved as a thing. So he paid the price for her; and then he handed her her papers of freedom. She did not even understand. "You are free", he said to her gently. "Free?" she said. "Can I go wherever I want to go now?" "Indeed you can", he said. "Then," she said, "if I am free to go anywhere I will stay with you and serve you until I die." Legally she was free; but love and gratitude had bound her in a new and willing service.

The absolute mastery of Jesus Christ is the inevitable consequence of his absolute love. The absolute obedience which we are bound to give him is the response of the heart to the love of him who loved us and gave himself for us.

The Plain Man Looks at the Apostles' Creed, p. 67

O God, our Father, we know that every day comes to us from thee filled with new opportunities; and we know that today will be like that.

We know that today will bring us the opportunity to do some useful work, and to justify our existence in the world; help us to do that work with all our might.
We know that today will bring us the opportunity to learn something new, and to add something to the store of our knowledge; help us to seize that opportunity.
We know that today will bring us the opportunity to witness

30

for thee, and to show on whose side we are; help us fearlessly to bear that witness.

We know that today will bring us an opportunity to lend a helping hand to those whose need is greater than our own; help us to be among our fellowmen as they who serve.

We know that today will bring us the opportunity to come closer to each other and nearer to thee; grant that we may so take that opportunity that, when the evening comes, we may be bound more firmly in comradeship to one another, and in love to thee: through Jesus Christ our Lord. Amen.

The Plain Man's Book of Prayers, p. 58

"I WROTE IT"

My father had a story he loved to tell. There was a girl near where we used to live who was suffering from an incurable disease and who was slowly and painfully dying. He used from time to time to visit her. On one occasion he took with him a very lovely little book of comfort for those in trouble written by an anonymous author. He gave it to her. "I thought", he said, "you might like to see it, and that it might help you." "I know this book", she said. "Have you got it already?" my father asked. She smiled and answered quietly: "I wrote it." Out of the furnace of affliction there had come, not only peace for herself, but also the power to help others. Even in the sorest day and even when all earthly help is gone the Christian can still say: "I am sure that neither death, nor life, nor angels, nor principalities, nor things present, nor things to come,

31

nor powers, nor height, nor depth, nor anything else in all creation, will be able to separate us from the love of God in Christ Jesus our Lord'' (Romans 8:38, 39).

Prayers for Help and Healing, p. 17

O God, somehow nowadays I am always tired. I go to sleep tired and I get up still tired.

Things take longer than they used to take, and I get behind with my work, and with the things I ought to do.

I come home tired, and that makes me cross and bad-tempered and irritable and impatient with my own family and my own people.

Everything has become an effort and a labour.

O God, help me to keep going, and help me to find something of the rest which you alone can give. Refresh me with your presence, and give me back the joy of living and the thrill of working: through Jesus Christ my Lord. Amen.

More Prayers for the Plain Man, p. 107

WORSHIP

For the Christian the Lord's Day should be used for worship. The word ''worship'' is a very wide word. Worship is worth-ship, and to worship is to confess and to experience the supreme worth of God. It is through some means or other to find the presence of God, and through that discovery to find the inspiration and the strength to live a life which is fit for the presence of God. William Temple's definition of worship places worship in the wider context which it ought to have. "To worship", Temple wrote, "is to quicken the conscience by the holiness of God, to feed the mind with the truth of God, to purge the imagination by the beauty of God, to open the heart to the love of God, to devote the will to the purpose of God."

We must clearly and willingly admit that there are many ways to worship. However difficult it is for the conventional religious mind to recognize it or to admit it, the church is not the only place in which worship in the real sense of the word is possible.

There are those for whom nature itself is the cathedral of God. Wordsworth writes of this experience of nature in "Lines composed a few miles above Tintern Abbey":

> I have felt
> A presence that disturbs me with the joy
> Of elevated thoughts; a sense sublime
> Of something far more deeply interfused.
> Whose dwelling is the light of setting suns,
> And the round ocean and the living air,
> And the blue sky, and in the mind of man.

There is no doubt that this is a description of worship, and unquestionably a man can worship in nature; it would be strange if we could not meet God in the world that God has made.

A man can worship in music. When Handel was asked how he had succeeded in writing the music of his *Messiah*, he answered: "I saw the Heavens open, and God sitting on his great white throne", and it is just that same experience that music can bring to some.

A man can worship in beauty. F. R. Barry, in his life of that great bishop, Mervyn Haigh, repeats a story about

Haigh that Dean Hedley Burrows told him. Burrows said that, when he was Dean of Hereford, Mervyn Haigh came to see him on one occasion. Burrows goes on: "He [Haigh] took me into the cathedral and led me to a certain point in the north nave aisle from which he could see the fifteenth-century vaulting in the south transept, and he said, 'It was that light which decided me to be ordained'." It was through beauty that God spoke to Mervyn Haigh.

It may well be that in this modern world a man may find his worship in the services that come to him on the air on radio and television. One of the strangest experiences in broadcasting is that, if one is taking part in a well-established programme which has been running perhaps for many years, a programme such, for instance, as the *People's Service*, one is acutely aware of an unseen fellowship; there is the clear consciousness that one is in the midst of a worshipping community which one cannot see but which one can vividly and intensely feel.

It may well be true that for the large majority of people worship must be a corporate act within a church; it may well be that at least some of us hesitate, or refuse, to recognize anything else as worship; but, if worship be the realization and the awareness of the presence of God, and of God's greatness, and the dedication of life to him, then there are many kinds of worship, and a man must find his own way to God. He must somehow use the Lord's Day to rediscover, to realize and to remember that God is very near.

The Plain Man's Guide to Ethics, pp. 46–47

O God, our Father, today we are remembering all the way by which thou hast brought us to this present hour, and we thank thee for every step of it.

We thank thee for every experience which has come to us, because we know that in it and through it all thou hast been loving us with an everlasting love.

For gladness and for grief; for sorrow and for joy; for laughter and for tears; for silence and for song:
We give thee thanks, O God.

That thou hast kept us in our going out and our coming in;
That thou hast enabled us to do our work, and to earn our living;
That thou hast brought us in safety to this present hour:
We give thee thanks, O God.

For any new things that we have learned, and for any new experiences through which we have passed;
If we can do our work a little better, and if we know life a little better;
For friends who are still closer to us, and for loved ones who are still more dear:
We give thee thanks, O God.

And today, as we remember the passing years, we thank thee most of all for Jesus Christ, the same yesterday, today and for ever. Help us to go on, certain that, as thou hast blessed the past, so the future is also for ever in thy hands: through Jesus Christ our Lord. Amen.

The Plain Man's Book of Prayers, p. 108

PARENTS

It is a common saying with more than a grain of truth in it, that there are no delinquent children; there are only delinquent parents. Dr George Ingle, in his book *The Lord's Creed*, quotes a circular issued by the police department of Houston, Texas, in the United States.

For Parents
How to make a child into a Delinquent:
12 Easy Rules

1. Begin at infancy to give the child everything he wants. In this way, he will grow up to believe the world owes him a living.
2. When he picks up bad language, laugh at him. This will make him think he's cute.
3. Never give him any spiritual training. Wait until he is 21, and then let him "decide for himself".
4. Avoid the use of the word "wrong". It may develop a guilt complex. This will condition him to believe later, when he is arrested for stealing a car, that society is against him and he is being persecuted.
5. Pick up everything he leaves lying around, books, shoes, clothes. Do everything for him so that he will be experienced in throwing all responsibility on others.
6. Let him read any printed matter he can get his hands on. Be careful that the silverware and drinking glasses are sterilized, but let his mind feast on garbage.
7. Quarrel frequently in the presence of your children. In this way they will not be too shocked when the home is broken up later.
8. Give a child all the spending money he wants. Never let him earn his own. Why should he have things as tough as you had them?

9. Satisfy his every craving for food, drink and comfort. See that every sensual desire is gratified. Denial may lead to harmful frustration.
10. Take his part against neighbours, teachers, policemen. They are prejudiced against your child.
11. When he gets into real trouble, apologize for yourself by saying, "I never could do anything with him."
12. Prepare for a life of grief. You will be likely to have it.

This is a warning document and for many parents it must strike home. There is literally nothing that can take the place of parental discipline and parental control. This is something that the parent owes the child. The child cannot honour the parent who is not honourable, and no parent who evades his or her own responsibility can ever expect to be honoured. Honour is something which has to be earned and deserved. It is not enough to look after the material and physical needs of the child. There is a mind and a character also to be formed, and they cannot be formed without that discipline which is the basis of all training.

The Plain Man's Guide to Ethics, pp. 57–58

Make me all through today, O God,
Obedient to my parents;
Respectful to my teachers;
Diligent in my work;
Fair in my games;
Clean in my pleasure;
Kind to those whom I can help;
True to my friends;
And loyal to you.
This I ask for Jesus' sake. Amen.

Prayers for Young People, p. 18

"YOU WERE THEN AND I'M NOW!"

There are too many homes in which parents and children are almost strangers to each other. The parent has nothing to say to the child; he is unable to communicate with his own young people. The children so often, if they want advice or guidance, do not turn naturally to their parents, but rather to someone else, to the teacher or the club leader.

This cleavage between the generations is no new thing. It seems to have been part and parcel of life all through history. Here is a well known quotation: "The world is passing through troublous times. The young people of today think of nothing but themselves. They have no reverence for parents or old age. They are impatient of all restraint. They talk as if they knew everything, and what passes for wisdom with us is foolishness with them. As for the girls, they are forward, immodest and unwomanly in speech, behaviour and dress." That might have been written yesterday. In point of fact, it is an extract from a sermon preached by Peter the Hermit in 1274! One generation and the generation that went before it never really understood each other very well.

On the whole, a very large part of the blame for this estrangement must lie at the door of the older generation. It may well be that the centre of the whole situation is that older people find it very hard to accept the fact that things have changed, and that time has passed, and that life has moved on. Every generation is apt to think that life must stand still as it knows it – and that is precisely what life refuses to do.

Elinor Mordaunt, the novelist, tells of a thing her own daughter said. She, the mother, had said to the child: "I would never have been allowed to do that when I was your age." Whereat the child immediately answered: "But you must remember, Mother, that you were then and I'm now." It is the then and the now which cause all the trouble, unless the parent remembers that other times beget other manners, and that one generation is necessarily different from another.

The biggest step towards sympathetic understanding will come quite simply from the realization that we cannot expect our children to be the same as ourselves. This is not totally to exonerate the younger generation, for youth is characteristically impatient and intolerant, but it should be easier for those of us who are older than it is for youth out of our maturity to exercise the patience which will keep open the lines of communication between the generations.

The Plain Man's Guide to Ethics, pp. 57–58

O God, help me today to think of the feelings of others
　　as much as I think of my own.
If I know that there are things which annoy the people
　　with whom I live and work, help me not to do them.
If I know that there are things which would please them,
　　help me to go out of my way to do them.
Help me to think before I speak, so that I may not thought-
　　lessly or tactlessly hurt or embarrass anyone else.
If I have to differ with anyone, help me to do so with
　　courtesy.
If I have to argue with anyone, help me to do so without
　　losing my temper.
If I have to find fault with anyone, help me to do so with
　　kindness.
If anyone has to find fault with me, help me to accept
　　it with a good grace.
Help me all through today to treat others as I would

wish them to treat me: through Jesus Christ my Lord.
Amen.

More Prayers for the Plain Man, p. 22

THE GATEWAY TO ETERNAL LIFE

Death is a universal fact of life. Birth and death are the
two great experiences through which every man must go,
and from which none is exempt. But there are different
attitudes to death. An American journalist set down as the
first article in his personal creed: "Never to allow myself
to think of death." But whether or not a man will allow
himself to think of death, death will force itself upon his
attention. There were certain principles which the famous
chancellor Sir Thomas More was not prepared to abandon,
and it was fairly clear that his fidelity to them would provoke
the king's displeasure and so result in his own death. He
seemed to be quite unaware of the danger of his position.
Once the Earl of Norfolk reminded him how close he walked
to death. Sir Thomas answered: "Then in good faith
between your grace and me there is but this, that I shall
die today, and you tomorrow." To him it was no more
than a universal fact that all men must die. Dr Johnson
wrote of a certain time in the life of Swift: "The thoughts
of death rushed upon him at this time with such incessant
importunity that they took possession of his mind, when
he first waked, for many hours together."

For some there is the fear of death. "Is not the fear of
death natural to man?" Boswell asked Johnson. "So much
so, sir," said Johnson, "that the whole of life is but keeping
away the thoughts of it." John Mactaggart was one of the

brilliant but short-lived Scottish men of letters. He once wrote: "Ever since the night on which my mother told me that there would come a day on which I would die and be covered with cold mould in a grave, I have been haunted with the thought." There are always those who are all their lives in bondage to the fear of death (Hebrews 2:15).

For some there has been the attraction of death as an escape from a life which has become too complicated or too exhausting to endure. Rupert Brooke was one of the great poets who perished all too young in the 1914–18 war. He had loved the beauty of the earth and the joy of living. Before he went overseas to France a lady gave him a little charm which she said would bring him luck and keep him safe. "Yes," he wrote back, "but what luck is we'll wait and see; I can well see that life might be great fun; but I can well see that death might be an admirable solution." For some death might seem to be the solution of all the problems. That almost legendary figure T. E. Lawrence once said: "O Lord, I am so tired. I want to lie down to sleep, to die. To die is best because there is no réveille." When life becomes intolerable, then death may look like the way out. "The gods", said the Stoics, "gave men life, but they gave them the even greater gift of being able to take their own lives away."

Finally, there are those who have faced death with joy, because they regarded death as the way to a still greater life. F. B. Meyer, a very short time before his death, wrote to a friend: "I have just heard to my surprise that I have only a few more days to live. It may be that before this reaches you I shall have entered the palace. Don't trouble to write; we shall meet in the morning." Hugh McKail was one of the most steadfast of the Covenanters. He was captured and condemned to death. He was to die in four days' time. He was led through the streets of Edinburgh to the Tolbooth, and the crowds wept for the pathos of his fate. But his own face shone. "Good news," he said, "I am within four days of enjoying the face of Christ." For him death was indeed the gateway to eternal life.

The Plain Man Looks at the Apostles' Creed, pp. 361–62

O God, our Father, we know that thou art afflicted in all our afflictions; and in our sorrow we come to thee today that thou mayest give to us the comfort which thou alone canst give.

Make us to be sure that in perfect wisdom, perfect love, and perfect power thou art working ever for the best.

Make us sure that a Father's hand will never cause his child a needless tear.

Make us so sure of thy love that we will be able to accept even that which we cannot understand.

Help us today to be thinking not of the darkness of death, but of the splendour of the life everlasting, for ever in thy presence and for ever with thee.

Help us still to face life with grace and gallantry; and help us to find courage to go on in the memory that the best tribute we can pay to our loved one is not the tribute of tears, but the constant memory that another has been added to the unseen cloud of witnesses who compass us about.

Comfort and uphold us, strengthen and support us, until we also come to the green pastures which are beside the still waters, and until we meet again those whom we have loved and lost awhile: through Jesus Christ our Lord. Amen.

The Plain Man's Book of Prayers, pp. 111–12

BELIEF

Belief has three elements in it in the Christian sense of the term.

First, it has unquestionably an intellectual element. We cannot believe unless we know the claims that Jesus Christ has made; we must in the first place *know about* him before we can *know* him. We must know the offer and the claims he makes, and we must know how they were substantiated by his life and actions.

Secondly, we must be convinced that these claims are true. Unless there is reasonable evidence for a claim we cannot really and truly believe that it is true.

Thirdly, there are, however, two ways in which evidence can come. It can come by the presentation of certain facts to the mind; or it can come through personal experience. It can come, perhaps will most frequently come, by a combination of both ways. It will come by the hearing of the facts first, and the experiencing of them afterwards. Our knowledge of Christ comes from the personal experience of what his presence and his fellowship can do for us when we accept his offers and his claims and commit the whole of life to them.

It is the belief which knows and experiences, and which commits itself to that knowledge and experience, which finds eternal life.

The Plain Man Looks at the Apostles' Creed, p. 376

O God, our Father, help us to learn the lessons that life is seeking to teach us.

Save us from making the same mistakes over and over again.

Save us from falling to the same temptations time and time again.
Save us from doing things that we should not do, until the doing of them has become a habit which we cannot break.
Save us from failing to realize our own weaknesses, and from refusing to see our own faults.
Save us from persisting in courses of action which we ought to have learned long ago can lead to nothing but trouble.
Save us from doing things which we know annoy other people.

Help us daily to grow stronger, purer, kinder.
Help us daily to shed old faults, and to gain new virtues, until, by thy grace, life becomes altogether new.

Hear this our morning prayer for thy love's sake. Amen.

The Plain Man's Book of Prayers, p. 80

THE FRUIT OF THE SPIRIT

Help me, O God, to sow in my life all the fruit of the Spirit:

Love, that I may live at peace with all men;
Joy, that I may be as happy as the day is long;
Peace, that I may never be worried and anxious;
Patience, that I may learn to wait upon events and to bear with people;
Gentleness, that I may always be kind;
Goodness, that I may be an example to all;
Fidelity, that I may always keep my promise and my word;

Meekness, that I may have every passion under strict
control;
Self-control, that I may be master of myself and so be fit
to serve others.

Grant me these things, O God; through Jesus Christ my
Lord. Amen.

USE IT OR LOSE IT

After a long time the master of these servants returned and
settled accounts with them. The man who had been given
the twelve hundred and fifty pounds came up with another
twelve hundred and fifty pounds. "Master," he said, "you
handed over twelve hundred and fifty pounds to me. I have
made a profit of another twelve hundred and fifty pounds."
"Well done!" his master said to him. "You have shown
yourself a good and trustworthy servant. Because you have
shown that I could depend on you to do a small job well,
I will give you a big job to do. Come and share your master's
joy."

The man who had been given the five hundred pounds
came up. "Sir," he said, "you handed over five hundred
pounds to me. I have made a profit of another five hundred
pounds." "Well done!" his master said to him. "You have
shown yourself to be a good and trustworthy servant.
Because you have shown that I could depend on you to do
a small job well, I will give you a big job to do. Come and
share your master's joy."

The man who had been given the two hundred and fifty
pounds came up. "Sir," he said, "I am well aware that you
are a shrewd and ruthless business man. I know that you
have a habit of letting someone else do the work and of then
taking the profits. I know you often step in and appropriate
the results of some enterprise which you did not initiate.
So I went and hid your two hundred and fifty pounds in

45

a hole in the ground, because I was afraid to take the risk of doing anything with it. Here you are! Your money is safe!" "You lazy good-for-nothing!" his master answered. "You knew very well that I have a habit of letting other people do the work and of then taking the profits. You knew very well that I often step in and appropriate the results of some enterprise which I did not initiate. That is all the more reason why you ought to have lodged my money with the bankers, and then, when I came home, I would have got my money back with interest. Take the two hundred and fifty pounds from him, and give it to the man who has two thousand five hundred pounds. For, if any man has much, he will be given still more, but, if any man has nothing, he will lose even what he has. Fling the useless servant out into outer darkness. There will be tears and agony there."

Matthew 25:14–30

I bind unto myself today
The power of God to hold and lead,
His eye to watch, his might to stay,
His ear to hearken to my need.
The wisdom of my God to teach,
His hand to guide, his shield to ward,
The word of God to give me speech,
His heavenly host to be my guard.

St Patrick's Breastplate, Stanza 1

More Prayers for Young People, pp. 76–77

"ALL SUNSHINE MAKES A DESERT"

There is no doubt that sorrow has a value of its own, and that it has a place in life which nothing else can take. There is always something missing in life, until sorrow has entered into life. There is an Arab proverb which says: "All sunshine makes a desert." It is told that once Elgar, the great musician, was listening to a young girl singing. She had a beautiful voice and a well-nigh faultless technique, but she just missed greatness. "She will be great", said Elgar, "when something happens to break her heart." There are things which only sorrow can teach.

It might well be said that sorrow is the source of the great discoveries in life. It is in sorrow that a man discovers the things which matter, and the things which do not matter. It is in sorrow that a man discovers the meaning of friendship and the meaning of love. It is in sorrow that a man discovers whether his fatih is a merely superficial ornament of life or the essential foundation on which his whole life depends. It is in sorrow that a man discovers God. "When you come to the bottom," said Neville Talbot, "you find God."

There is a deep sense in which it is literally true that sorrow has its own unique blessedness to give.

The Plain Man Looks at the Beatitudes, p. 26

O God,
The trouble about life just now
  is that I seem to have all the things
  which don't matter,
    and I seem to have lost all the things
    which do matter.

I have life;
   I have money enough to live on;
      I have a job to do;
but I am alone,
   and sometimes I feel that nothing
      can make up for that.
O God,
compel me to see the meaning of my faith.
   Make me realize that
      I have a hope as well as a memory;
   that the unseen cloud of witnesses is around me;
      that Jesus meant it when he said
      that he would always be with me.
And make me realize that
   so long as you leave me here
there is something that I am meant to do;
   and in doing it, help me to find
      the comfort and the courage
      that I need to go on.

Let me remember Paul's confidence:
   But we would not leave you ignorant, brethren, con-
   cerning those who are asleep, that you may not grieve as
   others do who have no hope. For since we believe that
   Jesus died and rose again, even so, through Jesus, God
   will bring with him those who have fallen asleep.
                                   1 Thessalonians 4:13, 14

'Midst pastures green he'll lead his flock,
   Where living streams appear,
And God the Lord from every eye
   Shall wipe off every tear.

                        Prayers for Help and Healing, p. 66

PERSEVERANCE

O God, give me the gift of perseverance.

If I fail in something the first time, help me to try and try again, until I succeed.

If I have to do something difficult, help me not to get discouraged, but to keep on trying.

If I find that results are slow to come, give me patience that I may learn to wait.

Help me to remember that the more difficult a thing is, the greater is the satisfaction in achieving it.

Help me to welcome every difficulty as a challenge and an opportunity for victory; through Jesus Christ my Lord. Amen.

JESUS IN HIS HOME TOWN

He went to Nazareth, where he had been brought up, and, as his habit was, he went into the synagogue on the Sabbath. He rose to read the scripture lesson. The roll containing the prophecies of Isaiah was handed to him. He unrolled the roll and found the passage where it is written:

> The Spirit of the Lord is upon me,
> because he has anointed me,
> to bring good news to the poor.
> He has sent me to announce to the prisoners
> that they will be liberated,
> and to the blind that they will see again,
> to send away in freedom
> those who have been broken by life,
> to announce that the year
> when the favour of God will be shown has come.

He rolled up the roll, and handed it back to the officer. He took the preacher's seat, and the eyes of everyone in the synagogue were fixed intently on him. "Today," he said to them, "this passage of scripture has come true, as you listened to it."

They all agreed that the reports that they had heard of him were true, and they were astonished at the gracious words he spoke. "Isn't this Joseph's son?" they said. He said: "You are bound to quote the proverb to me, 'Doctor, cure yourself.' Do here in your home country all that we have heard about you doing in Capernaum." He went on: "This is the truth I tell you, no prophet is accepted in his own native place. You know quite well that it is the fact that there was many a widow in Israel in Elijah's time, when the sky was closed for three and a half years, and there was a severe famine all over the country; but to none of them was Elijah sent; he was sent to a widow in Sarepta in Sidon. There was many a leper in Israel in the time of Elisha; and none of them was cured; but Naaman the Syrian was." The people in the synagogue were all enraged, when they heard him speak like this. They rose from their seats and hustled him out of the town. They took him to the brow of the hill on which their town is built, to hurl him down. But he walked straight through the middle of them, and went on his way.

Luke 4:16–30

O Lord God, when thou givest to thy servants to endeavour any great matter, grant us to know that it is not the beginning but the continuing of the same, until it be thoroughly finished, which yieldeth the true glory.

Sir Francis Drake

More Prayers for Young People, pp. 20–21

NEW LIFE

In the novel *Quo Vadis?* there is a picture of a young Roman called Vinicius. He is in love with a Christian girl, but because he is a pagan she will not return his love. Without her knowledge he followed her to the little secret gathering of the Christians, and there he heard Peter preach. As he listened something happened within him. He knew that Jesus Christ was the most important reality in life, but, "He felt that, if he wished to follow that teaching, he would have to place on a burning pile all his thoughts, habits and character, his whole nature up to that moment, burn them into ashes, and then fill himself with a life altogether different, and an entirely new soul." That is the demand of Christianity. The Christian does not say: "I am interested in Christ." He says: "For me to live is Christ" (Philippians 1:21). He does not say: "I would like to come to terms and to some arrangement with this Jesus." He says, "I surrender to Jesus Christ."

The Plain Man Looks at the Beatitudes, pp. 47–48

O God, our Father, save us this day from all the sins into which we so easily and so continually fall.

Save us from demanding standards from others which we never even try to satisfy ourselves.
Save us from being very easy on ourselves and very hard on others.
Save us from making excuses for things in ourselves which in others we would condemn.
Save us from being wide-open-eyed to the faults of others, and blind to our own.

Save us from taking for granted all that our loved ones do for us, and from never realizing how much they do and how much we demand.

Help us through this day to try to do to others what we would wish them to do to us, and so help us to fulfil the law of Jesus Christ. This we ask for thy love's sake. Amen.

The Plain Man's Book of Prayers, p. 42

THE MALADY OF NOT WANTING

It is the experience of life that, if a man desires a thing sufficiently, he will get it. If he is prepared to bend every energy, to sacrifice everything, to toil with sufficient intensity, to wait with sufficient patience, he will succeed in getting that on which he has set his heart. The great barrier to our becoming fully Christian is our failure to desire it enough, our deep-rooted unwillingness to pay the price of it, our fundamental desire not to upset life, but to keep it as it is. Luke gives us a different, and a complementary, version of this Beatitude: "Woe unto you that are full! for ye shall hunger" (Luke 6:25). That means: "Woe unto you who are satisfied, who are content with things as they are, who have no passionate desire for that which you have not got. You may live comfortably enough just now, but the day comes when you will discover that you have somehow missed the greatest things of all."

In *The Master of Ballantrae* Robert Louis Stevenson describes how the master left the ancestral home at Durrisdeer for the last time. He had not been a good man, but in that moment he was sad. He turned to his steward McKellar. "Ah, McKellar," he said, "do you think I have never a regret?" "I do not think", said McKellar, "that you could be so bad a man unless you had all the machinery to be a good one." "Not all," said the master, "it is there you are in error – the malady of not wanting."

The biggest barrier to the full entry into the Christian life is nothing other than the malady of not wanting.

The Plain Man Looks at the Beatitudes, pp. 48–49

O God,
It is very difficult to keep on hoping,
  when nothing seems to be happening.
And it is even more difficult
  when there seem to be more setbacks than progress.
Help me to have the hope
  that nothing can put out.
After all, even on the darkest night,
  no one ever doubts
    that the morning will come again;
and in the hardest winter
  no one ever doubts
    that spring is never far behind.
Help me to think
  of the skill you have given
    to those whose task it is to heal,
and of the essential toughness
  of this human body of mine.
Help me to remember
  that for you and with you
    nothing is impossible.
And help me to remember always
  that I have a hope
    that does not stop with this world,
      but goes on for ever.

Let me remember the Psalmist's confidence:
    Why are you cast down, O my soul,
    and why are you disquieted within me?
    Hope in God; for I shall again praise him,
    my help and my God.   *Psalm 43:5*

If thou but suffer God to guide thee,
    And hope in him through all thy ways,
He'll give thee strength, whate'er betide thee,
    And bear thee through the evil days;
Who trusts in God's unchanging love
Builds on the rock that nought can move.

Prayers for Help and Healing, p. 33

MAKING THE IMPOSSIBLE POSSIBLE

A short time ago I heard a very well known Glasgow minister tell of an incident which he had never forgotten.

More than thirty years ago now he had been at a service conducted by a very famous preacher, who for many years had occupied a great pulpit with the greatest distinction. After the service my friend went round to speak to the famous man. "Sir," he said, "when I think of the strain of preaching from this famous pulpit, I do not know how you have carried on all these years." The great preacher answered: *"In this job you do not carry on; you are carried on."*

My friend went on to say that at the time it had seemed to him almost a "slick" answer, but the years had taught him that it was nothing but the truth.

The Bible is full of this truth of the support of God. "Cast your burden on the Lord," said the Psalmist, "and he will sustain you" (Psalm 55:22). "When you pass through the waters, I will be with you," Isaiah heard God say, "and through the rivers, they shall not overwhelm you" (Isaiah 43:2). "The eternal God is your dwelling-place," said Moses, "and underneath are the everlasting arms" (Deuteronomy 33:27). Again and again the promise recurs.

There are three things to be said about this.

It is the experience of life that the promise is true. The plain fact is that many of us would bear witness that we have been made able to pass the breaking-point and not to break, that we have been enabled to come through that which we would have said to be impossible, if we had been told in advance that it was to happen.

But this promise is true only upon conditions. The first condition is that we must accept what happens. If we are in a state of bitterness and resentment, then the promise is not for us.

Carlyle dealt roughly with the lady who said: "I accept the universe." "By God," said Carlyle, "she'd better!"

Paul Sangster tells of an incident when his father went to visit a girl in hospital who was going blind, and whom no human skill was able to help. "Mr Sangster," Jessie said, "God is going to take my sight away." For a little while Sangster did not answer. Then he said, "Don't let him, Jessie. Give it to him." "What do you mean?" she asked. "Try to pray this prayer," he answered: " 'Father, if for any reason I must lose my sight, help me to give it to you.' "

You remember Job in the midst of the disasters which smote him: "The Lord gave, and the Lord hath taken away; blessed be the name of the Lord" (Job 1:21).

Before God's promise can come true, we have to accept that which happens to us. This is not to say that all sorrow and suffering and pain and disaster are the will of God. In many cases they are not; they are the result of the sin and the folly and the ignorance of man. But whatever happens, and however it happens, it has to be accepted before it can be transformed.

There is a second condition. We have to try to do our best with, and in, any situation in which we are involved. Acceptance does not mean that we sit down passively and do nothing whatever about a situation. It does not mean that we abandon the struggle to face life with gallantry and with efficiency. It means that what we can do, we will do.

No one ever gets anywhere by running away from life; however difficult life may be we still have to stand up to it. No one ever achieves anything by refusing to help himself.

Suppose health be lost, there is something we can do to pick up the threads again.

Suppose devastating sorrow comes, there is something we can do to get through the terrible days.

Suppose crushing disappointment comes, and hopes are dead, there is something left out of which to rebuild.

Suppose some sin or folly or mistake wrecks life, there is something still left to be salvaged from the wreckage.

It is always true that God helps those who help themselves; and it is also true that God is helpless to help those who refuse to be helped.

When a man faces things in all their agony, God comes in and makes the impossible possible.

In the Hands of God, pp. 138–40

O God, I know how apt I am to put things off.

Sometimes it is because I am too lazy to do them. Sometimes it is just because I am afraid to do them. Sometimes it is because I just can't make up my mind, and I shilly-

56

shally, and can't make a decision. Sometimes it is because I say to myself that tomorrow will be time enough.

I know that I have got into this bad habit, and I know that it causes trouble for myself and for other people, and I am only too well aware that because of it things that ought to have been done have never been done – and some of them can never be done at all now.

O God, help me to do better.

Help me to remember that for all I know tomorrow may never come.

Give me resolution to make up my mind, and strength and courage to act on my decision.

Help me never to leave until tomorrow what I ought to do today; and help me within each day to do the tasks and to make the decisions which the day demands.

Hear this my prayer for your love's sake. Amen.

More Prayers for the Plain Man, p. 115

THE HANDWRITING OF THE MAKER OF THE UNIVERSE

It is true that nature can be red in tooth and claw; it is true that man's pollution can defile nature; but God is there. Millais, the famous artist, tells how he came to see nature. His father, an old countryman, would take him out towards evening, and they would lie beside the cornfield and watch the rabbits play and the corn sway like a wave of the sea beneath the breeze. One evening, as there came upon the world a sunset of unutterable beauty, the old man rose, faced the splendour of the dying sun, took off his cap, and said softly: "My son, it is God." There would be no more pollution and no more destruction and no more desecration, if men would learn to reverence not only God, but also his handiwork.

Carlyle wrote: "He who in any way shows us better than we knew before that a lily of the fields is beautiful, does he not show it us as an effluence of the Fountain of all Beauty; as the *handwriting*, made visible there, of the great Maker of the Universe? He has sung for us, made us sing with him, 'a little verse of a sacred Psalm'."

The Lord is my Shepherd, p. 106

O God, our Father, before we go out on the duties and the tasks of this day, we ask thee to direct, to control, and to guide us all through its hours.

Grant that today we may never for one moment forget thy presence.

Grant that we may take no step, and that we may come to no decision, without thy guidance, and that, before we act, we may ever seek to find thy will for us.

Be on our lips, that we may speak no evil word.

Be in our eyes, that they may never linger on any forbidden thing.

Be on our hands, that we may do our own work with diligence, and serve the needs of others with eagerness.

Be in our minds, that no soiled or bitter thought may gain an entry to them.

Be in our hearts, that they may be warm with love for thee, and for our fellowmen.

Help us to begin, to continue, and to end this day in thee: through Jesus Christ our Lord. Amen.

The Plain Man's Book of Prayers, p. 43

DOING ORDINARY THINGS EXTRAORDINARILY WELL

The New Testament is quite sure that there is no better test of a man than the way in which he works. Again and again this is the keypoint of the parables of Jesus. All that a man has to show God is his work – and that does not mean *what* he has done so much as *how* he did it.

L. P. Jacks used to tell of an old Irish navvy who worked on the construction of railways long before the days of mechanical shovels and bulldozers and excavators, in the days when all they had was a shovel and a barrow. The old navvy's spade was so well used that it shone like stainless steel when he cleaned the mud off it at night. Some one once asked him jestingly: "Well, Paddy, what will you do when you die and when God asks you what you have to say for yourself?" "I think", said Paddy, "that I'll just show him my spade." L. P. Jacks was the author of many books, and he wrote his manuscripts by hand. When he wrote he always wore an old tweed jacket, and the right cuff of the jacket was worn away with rubbing against the desk as he wrote. "If it comes to that," Jacks used to say, "I think I'll show God the cuff of my jacket."

Work is the test – not the importance of the work from the prestige point of view, but the fidelity with which it is done. It has been truly said that God does not so much need people to do extraordinary things as he needs people who do ordinary things extraordinarily well.

Ethics in a Permissive Society, pp. 92–93

O God, I know that you like a good workman, and I
    don't think that I have been very good today.
I am remembering now
    Things I haven't done at all;
    Things I have left half-done and unfinished;
    Things I didn't do very well, not nearly as well as
        I could have done them;
    Things I did with a grudge;
    Things I put off, and things I refused to do.
Forgive me for all bad workmanship, and help me to do
    better tomorrow; through Jesus Christ my Lord.
    Amen.

Prayers for Young People, p. 91

"I'M GOING TO TREAT THEM AS IF THEY HAD NEVER BEEN AWAY"

The whole essence of the Gospel which Paul came to preach is that God, in his astounding mercy, treats the sinner as if he had been a good man. Instead of smashing the sinner, he welcomes him with open arms. Instead of outpouring the mighty vials of his outraged holiness, he pours out the cleansing waters of his sacrificial love.

When the American Civil War was in progress, and when the South had rebelled against the North on the question of slavery, someone once asked Lincoln: "When this war is over, and when the South has been subdued and conquered, and has come back into the Union, how are you going to treat these rebellious southerners, what are you going to do to them?'' Back came Lincoln's answer: ''I am going to treat them as if they had never been away.'' That is precisely what Paul means by justification; he means that in that astonishing love, God treats men as if they had never been away.

We so often think of justification as a theological, and even a remote, conception; but the perfect picture of justification lies in the Parable of the Prodigal Son. The son has planned to come back with his confession of sin against heaven and his father, and with his request to be made a hired servant. He is never allowed to make that request (Luke 15:18, 19, 21). His father welcomes him back, not to the status of servant, but to the status of son, as if he had never been away.

A Sunday school teacher was once telling the story of the Prodigal Son to a class in a slum mission in Scotland. She told the story of the son's rebellion, of his terrible fate in the far country, of his resolution to come home. And she went on, ''What do you think his father would do to him when he got home?'' From that class of slum children, who knew life at its toughest, back came the immediate answer: ''Bash him!'' That is the natural answer; that is what anyone would expect; but that is the wrong answer, for the glory of God is that God justifies the ungodly. He treats the bad man as if he had been good.

The Mind of St Paul, pp. 59–60

O God, I will meet all kinds of people today; help me to help them all.

If I meet any who are sad,
   help me to comfort them, even if I can do no more than say a word of sympathy and shake their hand.

If I meet any who are depressed,
   help me to cheer them up, and to send them on their way happier because they met me.

If I meet any who are tempted,
   help me to help them to resist temptation by showing them an example, or by speaking a gentle word of warning to them.

If I meet any who are worried,
   help me to ease their anxiety as far as I can.

If I meet any who are overworked,
   help me to lend them a hand, if I possibly can, even if it means extra work for me, and even if I have to go a long way out of my way to do so.

If I meet any who are disgruntled and discontented,
   help me to help them to feel that things are not as bad as they think they are.

If I meet any who are happy,
   help me to share in their joy, and never to grudge it to them.

Make me able to enter into the mind and heart of all whom I meet today, and to bring joy and happiness wherever I go: through Jesus Christ my Lord. Amen.

More Prayers for the Plain Man, p. 84

THE REWARD MOTIVE

It is said that when a little Jewish boy was learning the alphabet, his teacher sometimes offered him a reward. The letters of the alphabet were written on a slate; and they were written, not with chalk or with slate-pencil, but in a mixture of flour and honey. The teacher would point at a letter and ask what it was and, if the boy could answer correctly, he was allowed to lick the letter off the slate! Learning for him was as sweet as honey. Learning the law was sweeter than honey and more precious than gold.

The Psalmist looked forward to his reward if he faithfully kept the law. Nowadays we are very suspicious of introducing the reward motive. It is told of an old saint that he said that he would like to obliterate the joys of Paradise and extinguish the flames of hell so that people might obey God simply for the sake of obeying and not for the sake of any reward. But the Bible is never afraid of the reward motive. Jesus said:

Truly, I say unto you, whoever gives you a cup of water to drink because you bear the name of Christ, will by no means lose his reward

Mark 9:41

Blessed are you when men hate you, and when they exclude you and revile you, and cast out your name as evil, on account of the Son of Man! Rejoice in that day, and leap for joy, for behold, your reward is great in heaven; for so their fathers did to the prophets

Luke 6:22, 23

If you do good to those who do good to you, what credit is that to you? For even sinners do the same. And if you lend to those from whom you hope to receive, what credit

63

is that to you? Even sinners lend to sinners, to receive as much again. But love your enemies, and do good, and lend expecting nothing in return; and your reward will be great, and you will be sons of the Most High

Luke 6:33–35

Paul said:

> for he will render to every man according to his works; to those who by patience in well-doing seek for glory and honour and immortality, he will give eternal life; but for those who are factious and do not obey the truth, but obey wickedness, there will be wrath and fury. There will be tribulation and distress for every human being who does evil, the Jew first and also the Greek, but glory and honour and peace for everyone who does good, the Jew first and also the Greek. For God shows no partiality

Romans 2:6–11

The Bible does not shirk the reward motive, and why should it? Unless a thing is good for something, it is good for nothing.

The Lord is my Shepherd, pp. 116–17

Forgive me, O God, for everything in which I have failed today.
Forgive me for
    Losing my temper when I should have controlled it;
    Allowing my tongue to run away with me when I should have kept quiet;
    Allowing myself to have bitter feelings about someone else;
    Refusing to listen to good advice and for resenting correction when I deserved it.
Forgive me for
    Failing to do things as well as I could have done them,

Failing to finish the tasks I should have finished;
Failing to work my hardest at my lessons and my work,
and to play my hardest at my games.
Forgive me for everything that I meant to do and failed to
do, and for everything that I meant not to do and did.
This I ask for Jesus' sake. Amen.

Prayers for Young People, p. 75

HOW TO GROW OLD GRACEFULLY

When I was in London at New Year time, I was just about to cross a busy street when a hand was laid on my arm. It was a little old lady carrying a shopping bag. "Will you take me across the street?" she asked. "I'm too nervous nowadays to cross by myself." So I took her by the arm and helped her across the street. When we got to the other side she thanked me. I was just turning to leave her when she turned to look at me again. "*Never grow old*", she said, and vanished in the crowd on the busy pavement.

So this was her advice. She found old age so frightening, so humiliating and so generally unpleasant that her word to me was "Never grow old". There are many things to be said about that advice.

First and foremost, it is impossible advice. You may stop many things in this life and this world, but you cannot stop the years. You may keep it at bay for long enough, but you cannot stop the slow decay of bodily strength and the slow deterioration of the physical faculties. No man has yet discovered the elixir of perpetual youth. Carefulness will delay the process, but in the end it cannot stop it. The old lady's advice begins with the handicap of being impossible.

It is not only impossible advice; it is bad advice. Impossible advice is always bad advice, for it can only lead to frustration in those who try to take it. This is particularly so in the matter of which we are thinking. "There are so few," said Richard Steele, "who can grow old with a good grace." There are few more embarrassing sights than the sight of someone who is old trying to be young. There is nothing lovely in the sight of someone who is old, dressing, talking, acting, speaking in a deliberate attempt to appear young. You can say few more damaging things, for example, about a woman than to draw attention to this weakness. There are few more valuable abilities in life than the ability to accept things as they are, and any wise person accepts the years without any resentment at all, for any wise person knows that it is possible to live in the attitude that the best possible age in life is exactly the age you happen to be.

And this means that the advice not to grow old is mistaken advice, for there is another side to the question and another aspect to the balance-sheet. Perhaps Robert Browning's best-known stanza is:

> Grow old along with me!
> The best is yet to be,
> The last of life, for which the first was made:
> Our times are in His hand
> Who saith "A whole I planned,
> Youth shows but half; trust God: see all nor be afraid.

Seen in the Passing, pp. 70–71

O God,
It seems like yesterday
   that I went out to work for the first time;
and now I haven't much longer to go,

66

and I'm well over the halfway line.
I can't shut my eyes to the fact
   that I'm getting older.
Physically, I get more easily tired,
   and any effort becomes more and more of an effort.
Mentally, I'm slower;
   I can't work for so long at a time;
      and concentration is more difficult.
First and foremost, help me to realize quite clearly
   what I can do and what I can't do,
   and to accept my necessary limitations.
And then help me to be thankful
   for all that the years have given me,
      and for all the experience that
      life has brought me.
Help me to use what is left to me of life
   wisely and well;
for time is short now,
   and I dare not waste any of it.

Let me remember what the prophet said:
   Your old men shall dream dreams,
   And your young men shall see visions.   *Joel 2:28*

Long as my life shall last,
   Teach me thy way!
Where'er my lot be cast,
   Teach me thy way!
Until the race is run,
Until the journey's done,
Until the crown is won,
   Teach me thy way!

Prayers for Help and Healing, p. 54

67

"THEY'RE MAKIN' ROADS THAT LEAD TO NOWHERE!"

In his book, *An Arrow into the Air*, John H. Withers has a quotation from Gerald Healy's play, *The Black Stranger*. It comes from the days of the Irish potato famine in 1846. At that time as part of the relief work men were set to making roads which had no purpose whatever. It was simply to give them some work to do. One day in that desperate situation Michael comes home to his father, and says with a kind of poignant disillusionment: "They're makin' roads that lead to nowhere!" When we confess our ignorance, an ignorance which even Jesus shared, of dates and times; when we abandon all the Jewish imagery and pictures, which by this time have become only fantastic; when we strip the doctrine of the Second Coming down to its bare essentials; we are left with this tremendous truth – the doctrine of the Second Coming is the final guarantee that life can never be a road that leads to nowhere; it is a road which leads to Christ.

The Mind of St Paul, p. 173

O God, help me all through today
   To do nothing to worry those who love me;
   To do nothing to let down those who trust me;
   To do nothing to fail those who employ me;
   To do nothing to hurt those who are close to me.

Help me all through this day
   To do nothing which would be a cause of temptation to

someone else or which would make it easier for
someone else to go wrong;
Not to discourage anyone who is doing his best;
Not to dampen anyone's enthusiasms, or to increase
anyone's doubts.

Help me all through this day
To be a comfort to the sad;
To be a friend to the lonely;
To be an encouragement to the dispirited;
To be a help to those who are up against it.

So grant that others may see in me something of the
reflection of the Master whose I am and whom I seek to
serve.

This I ask for your love's sake. Amen.

More Prayers for the Plain Man, p. 28

THE ESSENTIAL GRACE

James Moffatt, in his book *Grace in the New Testament*, has
succinctly laid it down that the very essence and centre of
Pauline faith and religion can be summed up in one brief
sentence: ''All is of grace, and grace is for all.'' For Paul
grace is the essential grace.

We must begin by noting two general facts about grace.
These two facts are not exclusively Pauline; they belong to
the very nature of the idea of grace. We shall have to return
to them more fully, but at the moment we state them briefly.

First, grace is in essence a lovely thing. The Greek word
for grace is *charis*, and *charis* can mean *physical beauty*,

everything that is contained in the word *charm*. Grace always moves in the realm of winsomeness, of loveliness, of attractiveness, of beauty and of charm. The word has in it all the beauty of holiness. There are certain Christian terms which inevitably have in them an idea and an atmosphere of sternness and of severity. But grace, in the Christian sense, is a thing of such surpassing beauty that the heart bows down in wondering adoration before it. There is an old hymn which has the line: "Grace 'tis a charming sound", and there is a world of truth there.

Second, grace had always in it the idea of a gift, which is completely free and entirely undeserved. The ideas of grace and merit are mutually exclusive and completely contradictory. No one can earn grace; it can only be humbly, gratefully and adoringly received. Grace is something which is given, as we say, *gratis*. The fundamental idea of grace is a gift, given out of the sheer generosity of the giver's heart, a gift which the receiver could never have earned and could never have deserved by any efforts of his own.

The Mind of St Paul, p. 117

O God, give me all through today
> Grace willingly to say Yes, when I am asked to help someone else;
> Strength resolutely to say No, when I am tempted or persuaded to do anything that is wrong;
> Patience to say to myself Wait, when I am in too big a hurry;
> Resolution to say Now, when I am inclined to put off till some future time what should be done today;
> Obedience to say to you, Lord, What do you want me to do? in every choice which comes to me today.

Hear this my prayer through Jesus Christ my Lord. Amen.

Prayers for Young People, p. 80

"SHE HATH DONE WHAT SHE COULD"

It was near the end of Jesus' life and he was in the house of Simon the leper at Bethany, and there was a woman who loved Jesus for what he had done for her. All she had was an alabaster box of ointment, and she came and she anointed him with it. And there were some there who said that this was a foolish and a wasteful thing to do.

But Jesus paid her the biggest compliment you can pay anyone. He said: "Don't worry and criticize her. *She hath done what she could*" (Mark 14:3–9). She offered what she had to offer, and she gave the world a moment of immortal loveliness which will live for ever.

I'm sure you remember the old story of the acrobat who became a Christian. He came into a cathedral and he knelt before a statue of the Virgin Mary. He wanted so much to offer something, but he was poor and he had nothing to give. Then he looked round to see that there was no one watching, and he began to offer all he had to offer – his somersaults, his handstands, his acrobatic tricks.

When he had finished his routine he knelt there, and – the legend says – the Virgin stepped down from her statue and gently wiped the sweat from his brow. He offered what he had to offer.

What a Church we could make it be if people offered what they had to offer. *Jesus does not want what we haven't got; he wants what we have got.* Maybe we have a voice – and there is a church choir which could use it. Maybe we can teach a little – and there is a Sunday school which could use that. Maybe we have some skill or craft – and there's a job on the church buildings to be done which could use that.

We've got a home; and there are lonely people in our town. Jesus could use that home if we offered it to him, and if we were given to hospitality. Maybe there is a new housing area around our church or in our district; it's a big job to visit all these people and to give them an invitation to worship. We've got an evening or two to spare; the church could use that evening for a visit or two.

Maybe we've got a car, and there's an old person who could be doing with a lift to church, who maybe can't get to church any other way. Jesus could use that car.

There is a Scottish international football player who gave his church what he had to offer. What about us doing the same?

In the Hands of God, pp. 137–38

Give me, O God, a will that is strong and steady.
Help me
    Not to give up so easily,
      but to stick at things until I succeed in doing them;
    Not to be so easily annoyed,
      but to keep calm, and to take things as they come;
    Not to be so easily led,
      but to be able to stand alone, and, if necessary, to say
      No, and to keep on saying No;
    Not to lose interest so quickly,
      but to concentrate on everything I do,
      and to finish everything I begin.
Give me a will strong enough always to choose the right,

and never to be persuaded to anything that is wrong;
through Jesus Christ my Lord. Amen.

Prayers for Young People, p. 93

FOR A BIRTHDAY

O God, today another year of life is finished and another
  year of life has begun.
Thank you for bringing me safely through another year.
Grant that I may not only be a year older, but also a year
  wiser.
Help me to profit by experience, so that I may not make the
  same mistakes over and over again.
O God, at the end of one year of life and at the beginning
  of another, I cannot help remembering all that I meant
  to do and to be in the year that is just past, and how little
  I have actually done. Help me in this incoming year really
  to carry out my resolutions and intentions, so that when
  I come to the end of it there may be no regrets; through
  Jesus Christ my Lord. Amen.

More Prayers for Young People, pp. 124–25

THE PASSING YEARS

Lord, thou hast been our dwelling place
  in all generations.
Before the mountains were brought forth,
  or ever thou hadst formed the earth and the world,
  from everlasting to everlasting thou art God.

Thou turnest man back to the dust,
  and sayest, "Turn back, O children of men!"

For a thousand years in thy sight
  are but as yesterday when it is past,
  or as a watch in the night.

Thou dost sweep men away; they are like a dream,
  like grass which is renewed in the morning:
in the morning it flourishes and is renewed;
  in the evening it fades and withers.

For we are consumed by thy anger;
  by thy wrath we are overwhelmed.
Thou hast set our iniquities before thee,
  our secret sins in the light of thy countenance.

For all our days pass away under thy wrath,
  our years come to an end like a sigh.
The years of our life are three score and ten,
  or even by reason of strength four score;
yet their span is but toil and trouble;
  they are soon gone, and we fly away.

Who considers the power of thy anger,
  and thy wrath according to the fear of thee?
So teach us to number our days
  that we may get a heart of wisdom.

Psalm 90:1–12

It is my birthday, Lord Jesus, my saviour, and I thank thee for giving me the wonderful gift of life. I pray thee that I may use my life rightly, that I may try to grow braver, kinder, wiser and truer year by year. I thank thee for all the joys of the past year, and pray thee to bless me through the coming one. Help me to conquer my faults and live more to thy glory. Grant me thy grace to help all those around me, and to try to make them happy.

Be with me step by step all through this new year, and keep me safe unto the end; for thy sake. Amen.

A Chain of Prayer Across the Ages

More Prayers for Young People, pp. 124–25

"THE SECRET SPLENDOUR OF OUR INTENTIONS"

In his autobiography H. G. Wells drew a contrast between "the secret splendour of our intentions" and the poverty of our achievements. "A man may be a bad musician," he says, "and yet be passionately in love with music." Thomas à Kempis said: "Man sees the deed, but God sees the intention." And that applies in both directions. God does not see only the mixed and impure motive that may lurk behind that which looks like a good deed; he also sees the longing for goodness and the love of goodness which lies behind the sins and the mistakes of life. Sir Norman Birkett, as he then was, the great lawyer and judge, looking back on the many criminals he had met, once said: "They are condemned to some nobility; all their lives long the desire for good is at their heels, the implacable hunter." Robert Louis Stevenson spoke of those who had made shipwreck of life "clutching the remnants of virtue in the brothel or on the scaffold". When David wished to build a house unto God, it was not given to him to do so – that was reserved for his son Solomon – but nevertheless God said to him: "Thou didst well that it was in thine heart" (1 Kings 8:18).

The Plain Man Looks at the Beatitudes, p. 50

O God, I know quite well that I bring most of my troubles on myself.

> I leave things until the last minute, and then I have to do them in far too big a hurry to do them properly, and so I often come to school with lessons half-learned and work half-done.

> I don't spend all the time I ought to spend in work and in study, although I always mean to.

> I get angry and impatient far too easily, and the result is that I upset myself and everyone else.

> I do things without thinking first, and then I am sorry I did them.

> I hurt the people I love most of all, and then – too late – I am sorry for what I said or did.

It is not that I don't know what is right. I do know – but the trouble is that I mean to do it and then don't do it.

I need your help to strengthen me and to change me.

Please help me to do what I cannot do and to be what I cannot be by myself.

This I ask for your love's sake. Amen.

Prayers for Young People, p. 27

TOLERANCE

There is always a reason why a person thinks as he does think, and by entering into that person's mind and heart, and by seeing things with his eyes we could understand that reason, and tolerance would be much easier. John Wheatley was one of the famous Clyde-side Members of Parliament. He spoke like a fire-brand and a revolutionary, and was regarded as a rebel. He was once talking to King George the Fifth. The king asked him why he was so violent an agitator. Wheatley quite simply told the king something of the slums of which he knew so much, and of the life that people had to live there, and of the spectre of unemployment, and the life of the working-man. When he had finished, the king said quietly: "If I had seen what you have seen, I too would be a revolutionary." The king had seen the world with Wheatley's eyes, and understood. Tolerance is only possible when we make the effort of self-identification with others.

The Plain Man Looks at the Beatitudes, p. 69

O God, grant that all through today I may never find any request for help a nuisance.

Help me never to find a child a nuisance,
   when he wants me to help him with his lessons,
   or play with him in his games.

Help me never to find a sick person a nuisance,
   if he would like me to spend some time with him,
   or do some service for him.

Help me never to find someone who is old a nuisance,
   even if he is critical of youth,
   settled immovably in his ways,
   demanding of attention.

Help me never to find a nuisance anyone who asks me
   To show him how to do things;
   To help him in his work;
   To listen to his troubles.

Grant, O God, that I may neither be too immersed in work nor too fond of my own pleasure, that I may never be too busy and never too tired, to help those who need help, even if they are the kind of people who get on my nerves and whom I instinctively dislike.

Help me to help, not only when it is pleasant to help, but when help is difficult and when I don't want to give it: through Jesus Christ my Lord. Amen.

More Prayers for the Plain Man, p. 98

"PEACE I LEAVE WITH YOU, MY PEACE I GIVE TO YOU"

For us peace is largely a negative word; it tends to describe mainly the absence or the cessation of war and trouble. Even in a situation in which a land was devastated, in which cities were in ruins, and in which men, women and children were starving, if war came to an end, we would likely say that peace had returned. But for a Jew peace had a far wider meaning than that. The Greek word for peace is *eirene*, which translates the Hebrew word *shalom*. *Shalom* has two main meanings. It describes perfect welfare, serenity, prosperity and happiness. The eastern greeting is *Salaam*, and that greeting does not only wish a man freedom from trouble; it wishes him everything which makes for his contentment and his good. For the Jew peace is a condition of perfect and complete positive well-being. Second, *shalom* describes right personal relationships; it describes intimacy, fellowship, uninterrupted goodwill between man and man. It can easily be seen that peace does not describe only the absence of war and strife; peace describes happiness and well-being of life, and perfection of human relationships.

When the Psalmist prays that peace should be within the walls of Jerusalem (Psalm 122:7, 8), he is praying that every good blessing should descent upon the city and upon its citizens.

It would be true to say that the New Testament is the book of this peace. In it the word *peace*, *eirene*, occurs eighty-eight times, and it occurs in every book. One of the great characteristics of the New Testament letters is that they begin and end with a prayer for peace for those who are to read and to listen to them. Paul begins every one of his letters with the prayer that grace and peace may be on the people to whom he writes, and often the New Testament letters end with some such phrase as "Peace be to you all". When Jesus was leaving his disciples, as John tells the story, he said to them: "Peace I leave with you, my peace I give unto you" (John 14:27). J. S. Stewart has called that the last will and testament of Jesus. Of worldly goods and possessions Jesus had nothing to leave, but he left to men his peace.

The Plain Man Looks at the Beatitudes, pp. 82–83

O God, sometimes I begin to worry, especially when I sit at the end of the day and think.

I begin to worry about my work.
    Help me to know that with your help I can cope.

I begin to worry about money, and about making ends meet.
    Help me to remember that, though money is important, there are things that money cannot buy – and these are the most precious things of all.

I begin to worry about my health.
    Help me to remember that worrying makes me worse, and that trusting always makes me better.

I begin to worry about the things which tempt me.
Help me to remember that you are with me to help me
to conquer them.

I begin to worry about those I love.
Help me to do everything I can for them, and then to leave
them in your care.

Give me tonight your peace in my troubled heart: through
Jesus Christ my Lord. Amen.

More Prayers for the Plain Man, pp. 30–31

THE WALLS OF SPARTA

Sometimes the Church is likened to a *building*. You are God's
building, Paul writes to the Church at Corinth (1 Corinthians
3:9). Peter develops this building picture when he sees the
individual Christians as individual, living stones built into
the structure of a spiritual house of which the corner-stone
is Jesus Christ (1 Peter 2:4–7).

There are two great thoughts in the picture of the Church
as a building. First, it gives us the truth that in the Church
each individual Christian has a place, like the stones in a
house, and the removal of any injures both the beauty and
the strength of the structure. Secondly, it gives us the truth
that the whole structure will necessarily collapse if the
corner-stone is removed, and the corner-stone is Jesus
Christ. The Church is composed of people built into, and
held together by, Jesus Christ.

That picture of the Church reminds us of the saying of
the Spartan king. He had boasted that no nation in the world
had walls like Sparta. But when a visitor came to visit Sparta

he saw no walls at all, and asked the Spartan king where the walls were. The Spartan king pointed at his body-guard of magnificent Spartan soldiers: "These", he said, "are the walls of Sparta, and every man of them a brick." In exactly the same way, the Christian is the living stone built into the structure of the Church.

The Plain Man Looks at the Apostles' Creed, pp. 272–73

O God, our Father, we thank thee for everything which brings us nearer to thee.

We thank thee for thy book, to tell us of thy dealings with thy people, and to set before us the deeds and words of our blessed Lord in the days of his flesh.

We thank thee for the music and the poetry of the psalms and the hymns we sing, and for all the memories which they awaken.

We thank thee for the open door of prayer which no man can ever shut.

We thank thee for this day with its call to lay aside the things of earth and to enter into thy house.

We thank thee for the preaching of thy word, to comfort our hearts and to enlighten our minds.

We thank thee for the sacraments of thy grace to be the channels of the love divine.

Open our minds and hearts today, that in it and in its worship we may receive the precious things which thou art waiting to give: through Jesus Christ our Lord. Amen.

The Plain Man's Book of Prayers, p. 90

"THE GOOD THAT I WOULD, I DO NOT; BUT THE EVIL WHICH I WOULD NOT, I DO"

It is a fact of experience that every man is at least to some extent a split personality. It was the Jewish belief that in every man there were two natures, the good nature which drew him up, and the evil nature which dragged him down. It was as if a good angel stood at his right hand beckoning him to goodness, and an evil angel stood at his left hand beckoning him to evil. Life has been described as "an endless war of contrarieties". This is the struggle of which Paul wrote so movingly in the seventh chapter of Romans. "The good that I would, I do not; but the evil which I would not, I do" (Romans 7:19). There was a war in his members between two laws, the one urging him to goodness, the other enticing him to sin. This was the picture which Plato drew of human nature. He pictured the soul as a charioteer. Yoked to the chariot there are two horses. The one horse is wild and untamed; the other is gentle and under control. The name of the first horse is passion, and the name of the second horse is reason; and somehow the soul has to control them and to make them run in double harness. A. E. Housman in one of his verses vividly expresses the universal human experience:

> More than I, if truth were told,
> Have stood and sweated hot and cold,
> While through their veins, like ice and fire,
> Fear contended with desire.

Robert Burns was well aware of the wreckage which he so often made of life. "My life", he said, "reminded me of a ruined temple; what strength, what proportion in some parts, what unsightly gaps, what ruin in others."

Studdert Kennedy describes the feelings of a soldier in the first world war. The public tried to treat him as a hero; the padre insisted on treating him as a hell-deserving sinner.

> Our padre says I'm a sinner,
> And John Bull says I'm a saint,
> And they're both of them bound to be liars,
> For I'm neither of them, I ain't.
> I'm a man, and a man's a mixture,
> Right down from his very birth,
> For part of him comes from heaven,
> And part of him comes from earth.
> There's nothing in him that's perfect;
> There's nothing that's all complete.
> He's nobbut a great beginning
> From his head to the soles of his feet.

Every man well knows that he is a mixture. We know that we are capable at one time of an almost saintly goodness, and at another time of an almost devilish evil. We know that at one time we are capable of an almost sacrificial kindness, and at another of an almost heartless callousness. We know that sometimes the vision of goodness fills our horizon, and that other times the unclean and evil desire has us at its mercy. We are part ape and part angel.

The Plain Man Looks at the Beatitudes, pp. 82–83

O God, give me a sense of responsibility.
Keep me
    From doing things without thinking;

From leaving an untidy mess behind me wherever I go;

From being carelessly or deliberately destructive;

From not caring how much worry and anxiety I cause other people;

From not even beginning to realize all that I get, and all that is done for me, and all that it costs to give it to me;

From failing to grasp the opportunities which are offered to me;

From failing to realize the difference between the things which are important and the things which do not matter.

Help me

Always to use my time and my life wisely and well;

Always to be considerate of others;

Always to realize all that is done for me, and to show by my good and cheerful conduct that I am grateful for it.

Hear this my prayer, for Jesus' sake. Amen.

Prayers for Young People, p. 90

CHRIST BRIDGES THE GULF

Bishop Lesslie Newbiggin tells of an experience in his diocese in India. When the United Church of South India came into being, and when he became one of its bishops, he made an introductory tour of his diocese. At each village the Christian community came out to meet its bishop.

In one village the Christians were led by an extraordinary figure, clad in very aged RAF equipment, and carrying a stainless steel baton. With this baton he controlled, as it

84

were, his congregation. At a sign from him they knelt, and at another sign they rose. Bishop Newbiggin was staying with him when his story came out. His name was Sundaram.

At the beginning of the second world war he was preaching the Gospel in Burma. He was captured in the advance of the Japanese armies. He was taken to a guard-post. Everything he possessed was taken from him and he was bound and thrown into a corner. A Japanese officer came in. He went to the table where Sundaram's scanty belongings lay. He picked up the Tamil Bible. He knew no word of Tamil but he recognized it as a Bible. He held up his hand and traced on the palm the sign of the Cross and looked questioningly at Sundaram. Sundaram knew no word of Japanese, but he knew that the officer was asking if he was a Christian, and he nodded. The officer walked across to him, stood in front of him with his arms stretched out in the form of the Cross, cut his bonds, gave him back his belongings, and pointed to the door, bidding him to go. And, before Sundaram went out to freedom, the Japanese officer handed him as a token and memento his officer's staff; and that officer's staff was the stainless steel baton with which Sundaram directed his Indian congregation.

Here were two men who knew not a word of each other's language, two men from nations which were at war, two men between whom there stretched a gulf which was humanly speaking beyond bridging – and Christ bridged that gulf. Jesus Christ reached out across the divisions and in Christ brought two men together again.

The Plain Man Looks at the Beatitudes, pp. 91–92

Lord Jesus, help me to remember that you are always with
    me.
Help me to do nothing which it would grieve you to see,

and nothing which I would be ashamed to think that you
should see me doing.

When I am tempted, help me always to ask you for strength
to do the right thing and to resist the wrong thing.

When I don't know what to do, help me to turn to you and
ask you for your advice.

When I am frightened and lonely, help me to feel that you
are there, and to know that with you I don't ever need
to be afraid.

Help me to go through life with you as my Friend and my
Companion all the time.

This I ask for your love's sake. Amen.

Prayers for Young People, p. 56

"RAISE THE STONE AND YOU WILL FIND ME; CLEAVE THE WOOD AND I AM THERE"

There is a very beautiful saying of Christ which is one of
the unwritten sayings which do not appear in the New
Testament at all: "Raise the stone and you will find me;
cleave the wood and I am there." It means that, as the
mason works at the stone, as the carpenter handles the
wood, the Risen Christ is with him. The Resurrection means
that every way of life can be walked hand in hand with the
living Christ. The reservoir of the power of his presence is
open for every Christian to draw upon.

But the most uncompromising statement of the utter
necessity of the Resurrection is in 1 Corinthians 15:14–19.
There Paul writes: "If Christ be not risen, then is our
preaching vain, and your faith is also vain . . . If Christ

be not raised, your faith is vain; ye are yet in your sins. Then they also which are fallen asleep in Christ are perished. If in this life only we have hope in Christ, we are of all men most miserable.'' Why should that be so? What are the great truths which the Resurrection, and the Resurrection alone, guarantees and conserves? The Resurrection is the guarantee of four great truths.

It proves that *truth is stronger than falsehood*. In Jesus Christ God's truth came to men; men sought to eliminate, to obliterate, to destroy that truth, but the Resurrection is the final proof of the indestructibility of the truth of God.

It proves that *good is stronger than evil*. Jesus Christ was the incarnate goodness of God. The sin of man sought to destroy that goodness. But the Resurrection is the proof that goodness must in the end triumph over all that evil can do to it.

It is proof that *life is stronger than death*. Men sought to destroy the life of Jesus Christ once and for all; the Resurrection is the proof that the life which is in Christ cannot be destroyed – and the Christian shares that life.

It is the proof that *love is stronger than hate*. In the last analysis the contest in Jerusalem was a contest between the hatred of men and the love of God. Men took that love and sought to break it for ever on the Cross; but the Resurrection is the proof that the love of God is stronger than all the hatred of men, and can in the end defeat all that that hatred can do to it.

Unless we could be certain of these great truths life would be intolerable.

To Paul the Resurrection of Jesus Christ was neither simply a fact in history nor a theological dogma. It was the supreme fact of experience. To Paul the fact of the Resurrection meant the greatest thing in all the world; it meant that all life is lived in the presence of the love and of the power of Jesus Christ.

The Mind of St Paul, pp. 89–90

Lord Jesus, help me to walk with you all through today.

Give me today
  Something of the wisdom that was in your words;
  Something of the love that was in your heart;
  Something of the help that was on your hands.

Give me today
  Something of your patience with people;
  Something of your ability to bear slights and insults and
    injuries without bitterness and without resentment;
  Something of your ability always to forgive.

Help me to live in such a way today that others may know
that I began the day with you, and that I am walking with
you, so that, however dimly, others may see you in me.

This I ask for your love's sake. Amen.

More Prayers for the Plain Man, pp. 30–31

THE RESURRECTION

He would be a bold and reckless man who would say that
he knows everything about the Resurrection of Jesus Christ,
but, when we probe to the essential meaning of the fact and
of all the stories which have gathered round it, we come
to the certain truth that Jesus Christ is such that it is open
to those who know him and love him to experience his for
ever living presence and his for ever living power.

The basic meaning of the Resurrection is the liberation of
Jesus Christ. John Masefield in his play tells in imagination
how Procla, the wife of Pilate, sent for Longinus, the
centurion in charge of the crucifixion, and asked him what

had happened. "He was a fine young man," said Longinus, "but when we were finished with him he was a poor broken thing on the cross." "So you think", said Procla, "that he is finished and ended?" "No, madam, I do not", said Longinus. "He is set free throughout the world where neither Jew nor Greek can stop his truth."

We may argue for long enough about the details, and about how it happened. We may argue for long enough about the empty tomb and about the physical character of the Resurrection body of Jesus. In the last analysis these things are not important. What is important is that the Christian is sure that he possesses a Lord who is not a figure in history who lived and died and whose story we tell, but one whom we can daily meet and experience and who is alive for evermore, present to comfort and mighty to help.

For the Christian the Resurrection necessarily means two things: First, he never lives life alone. In every problem the Risen Christ is there to consult; in every effort he is there to help; in every sorrow he is there to comfort; on every dark road he is there to banish fear, and in the sunshine he is there to make joy doubly dear. He has at his side one who has fulfilled his promise to be with his people to the end of time and beyond.

Secondly, he has the knowledge that there is nothing he does which his Lord does not see, and nothing he says which his Lord does not hear. He has therefore in the memory of that presence an antiseptic against all evil, and a warning and an inspiration to make life fit for those eyes to see.

Whatever be the problems of the Resurrection, about which the historian and the theologian may argue, the Christian knows the certainty of the continued presence and power of his Lord, a presence and a power which even death cannot take away.

The Plain Man Looks at the Apostles' Creed, pp. 160–61

O God, our Father, we thank thee for this day which is
passing from us now.

For any glimpse of beauty we have seen;
For any echo of thy truth that we have heard;
For any kindness that we have received;
For any good that we have been enabled to do;
And for any temptation which thou didst give us grace to
overcome:
We thank thee, O God.

We ask thy forgiveness for anything which has spoiled and
marred this day.
For any word which now we wish that we had never
spoken;
For any deed which now we wish that we had never done;
For everything which makes us ashamed when we
remember it;
Forgive us, O God.

Eternal God, who givest us the day for work and the night
for rest, grant unto us, as we go to rest, a good night's
sleep; and wake us refreshed on the morrow, better able
to serve thee and to serve our fellow-men. This we ask,
through Jesus Christ our Lord.

The Plain Man's Book of Prayers, pp. 24–25

WHAT IS THE POINT?

Rusty, our bull-terrier, likes nothing better than to get into
the country. Give him a moor or a hillside and he is in his
glory. But of all things, he likes water best. Take him to the

seaside, and he will meet the waves one by one, the bigger the better.

Even more, he likes a shallow river or a burn. There, he seems to have one ambition – to remove all the stones from the bottom of it, and to lay them some considerable distance away on dry land. He sticks his head into the water, and nuzzles about on the bottom of the burn – I never can understand how he manages to go so long without breathing – and then emerges with a stone which he carries up the bank and carefully places on the ground fifty or a hundred yards away. *And he is back for more.*

He will do this for hours. I have seen him staggering out of burns with stones almost as big as himself; and, if he does find a stone he can't move, he nearly goes frantic. This afternoon, out in the country, Rusty spent almost two hours shifting stones from the bed of a burn.

Now Rusty is an intelligent dog – but I have always wished that he could tell me what's the point of all this. He never does anything with the stones; he simply goes on taking them out and laying them on the ground. It seems the most pointless proceeding anyone can imagine, but it is Rusty's idea of bliss.

What's the point of it? – that is what I would like to ask; and, when you come to think about it, it is a question one might ask of a great many people as well as of a Staffordshire bull-terrier.

What's the point of so much of our business and of our hurry and our worry and our effort and our anxiety? We strive so hard to get a little more money, to get a little further up the ladder – and what's the point of it all? What good is it really going to do us? We trouble about this and that and the next thing. Even if the things we fear happen, the heavens won't collapse, and, as a friend of mine often says, it will be all the same a hundred years from now.

We would do well to stand still sometimes and ask: "What's the point of what I'm doing?"

I do occasionally wonder about many of the arguments that go on in committees and presbyteries and all kinds of bodies. It seems hardly an exaggeration to say that we can get all hot and bothered about a comma. A trifle can be magnified into a matter of epoch-making principle. It is beyond doubt that we would save time and trouble and wear and tear, if before we started an argument we would say: "What's the point of it anyhow?"

I hope that I won't be misunderstood, if I say that there is a great deal of scholarship of which one is sorely tempted to ask: "What's the point of it?" There are many books which have undoubtedly taken years of research, and which, regarded as pure scholarship, are monuments of erudition, but what's the point of them?

Epictetus used to say: "Vain is the discourse of philosophy by which no human heart is healed." It is an interesting test – and, if it were applied, quite a number of erudite works would emerge as vanity.

Seen in the Passing, pp. 14–15

O God, I know that I am going to be very busy today. Help me not to be so busy that I miss the most important things.

Help me not to be too busy to look up and to see a glimpse of beauty in your world.

Help me not to be too busy listening to other voices to hear your voice when you speak to me.

Help me not to be too busy to listen to anyone who is in trouble, and to help anyone who is in difficulty.

Help me not to be too busy to stand still for a moment to think and to remember.

Help me not to be too busy to remember the claims of my home, my children and my family.

Help me all through today to remember that I must work my hardest, and also to remember that sometimes I must be still.

This I ask for Jesus' sake. Amen.

More Prayers for the Plain Man, p. 30

SERVICE

A week or two ago, work took me to a very famous university city in England, and there I was put up at a famous hotel. I arrived in time for dinner in the evening, and, of course, when I ordered dinner I gave the waiter my room number – and there are well over one hundred rooms in that hotel, and all were full.

Next morning I came down to breakfast, and the same waiter was on duty at the table at which I sat down. As I ordered breakfast, again I gave my room number. The waiter looked at me with a pained expression on his face. "Of course, I know your number, sir", he said. "You are one of our guests. You were in to dinner last night."

When I came out of the breakfast room, I was crossing the entrance hall, and the head porter came up to me. "Your mail, sir", he said, handing me a pile of letters. I had only seen him in the passing when I came into the hotel the night before, and yet he knew who I was out of the hundreds of people staying there.

Ten days or so later I told this story to a porter in another hotel as far north as that one was south, to which work had taken me, and he looked at me in surprise. "But, sir," he said, "that would happen in any decent hotel."

Now it seems there is nothing unusual in these happenings. But – and here is the point – in how many churches would it happen! In how many churches would a stranger be recognized by name on his second visit?

Many a person can attend for weeks, and not be spoken to, much less be addressed by name. Anyone who has found it out, will likely have forgotten it. One has a much better chance of being recognized in the crowd in a good hotel than he has in many churches.

In the Hands of God, pp. 42–43

O God, my Father, make me more appreciative of others.

Help me never to fail to say thanks for everything that is done for me, and never to take anything for granted, just because it comes to me unfailingly every day.

Help me always to be ready to speak a word of praise, whenever a word of praise is possible – and sometimes even when it is not possible.

Help me to be quick to notice things. Help me to be quick to see when someone is depressed and discouraged and unhappy. Help me to be quick to see it when someone is lonely and shy and is left out of things.

O Lord Jesus, all through today help me to see people with your eyes.

This I ask for your love's sake. Amen.

More Prayers for the Plain Man, p. 84

PRAYER IS NOT THE EASY WAY OUT

Prayer is not an easy way of getting things done for us. So many people think of prayer as a kind of magic, a kind of talisman, a kind of divine Aladdin's lamp in which in some mysterious way we command the power of God to work for us. Prayer must always remain quite ineffective, unless we do everything we can to make our own prayers come true. It is a basic rule of prayer that God will never do for us what we can do for ourselves. Prayer does not do things for us; it enables us to do things for ourselves.

Any wise parent knows that real parenthood does not mean doing things for the child; it means enabling the child to do things for himself. One of the great stories of history concerns Edward the First and his son the Black Prince. In battle the prince was sorely pressed. There were courtiers who came to the king to tell him that his son was up against it. "Is he wounded or unhorsed?" asked the king. When they said no, the king replied: "Then I will send him no help. Let him win his spurs."

To take the matter on a much more everyday level, it is much easier for a parent, when his child asks help with a school exercise, to do the exercise and then to allow the child to copy out the answer. But by that way the child will make no progress at all. By far the wiser way is to teach and to encourage the child to do it for himself. Prayer is not so much God doing things for us as it is we and God doing things together.

We cannot expect escape from prayer, and we cannot expect the easy way out. What we can expect is a strength not our own to do the undoable, to bear the unbearable and to face the unfaceable. What we can expect is that divine help in which everything becomes victory. "In the world ye shall have tribulation," said Jesus, "but be of good cheer; I have overcome the world" (John 16:33).

More Prayers for the Plain Man, p. 16

O God,
Help me not to waste my time. Don't let me always be in a hurry and a fuss, but help me to go quietly and without haste, filling every minute with the work which is given me to do.

Help me not to waste my strength. Help me to see quite clearly the things which matter and the things which don't matter. Give me a sense of proportion that I may not get all hot and bothered about things which are of no importance, and so make myself too tired and exhausted to do the things which really matter.

Help me not to waste my money. Don't let me be mean and miserly, but help me to spend wisely and to give generously, and to try to use everything I have, remembering that it belongs, not to me, but to you.

Above all, help me not to waste my life. Help me to use the talents you have given me, to seize the opportunities you are sending to me, so that some day you may be able to say to me: Well done!

You are the Lord and Master of all good life; hear this my prayer and help me to live well: through Jesus Christ my Lord. Amen.

More Prayers for the Plain Man, p. 118

GOING TO WORK FOR THE FIRST TIME

O God, bless me as I go out to work for the first time.
In my work help me always to do my best, so that I may
  be a workman who never has any need to be ashamed.
Help me to work equally hard whether I am watched or
  not, always remembering that you see me, and always
  trying to make my work good enough to offer to you.
Help me always to remember that Jesus worked in the
  carpenter's shop in Nazareth, and help me to be as good
  a workman as he was.

This I ask for you love's sake. Amen.

A GOOD WORKMAN

Remember Jesus Christ, risen from the dead, descended from David. This is what my gospel teaches. It is for the sake of that gospel that I am at present suffering, even to the length of being imprisoned as a criminal. But no one can put the word of God in prison. It is for the sake of God's chosen ones that I can pass the breaking-point and not break. I want them too to win that salvation which is ours because of what Christ Jesus has done for us, and with the glory that is eternal. It has been said, and said truly:

If we have died with him,
  we shall live with him;
if we endure,
  we shall reign with him;
if we deny him,
  he too will deny us;
if we are faithless,
  he remains faithful,
  for he cannot deny himself.

Keep on reminding them of all this. Charge them before God not to engage in pugnacious debates about verbal niceties. Debates like that are an unprofitable occupation, and do nothing but undermine the faith of the hearers. Do your best to present yourself to God as a man of sterling worth, a workman who has no need to be ashamed of his work, a sound expositor of the true word.

2 Timothy 2:8–15

Do thou thyself, O Lord, send out thy light and thy truth, and enlighten the eyes of our minds to understand thy divine Word. Give us grace to be hearers of it, and not hearers only, but doers of the Word, that we may bring forth good fruit abundantly and be counted worthy of the kingdom of heaven. And to thee, O Lord our God, we ascribe glory and thanksgiving, now and for ever. Amen.

Liturgy of the Greek Church

More Prayers for Young People, p. 63

"HE SIGNS HIMSELF 'PAUL'!"

There was a kirk which was looking for a minister. The vacancy committee was at the stage when it was sifting its way through the applications. The committee listened attentively as the clerk read them one by one.

All the candidates, with one exception, seemed to be gentlemen of the highest moral character – brilliant orators, tireless pastors, and experts at reviving flagging congregations and making misers glad to give.

The application which was different from the others went like this: "I have preached in a number of small churches, mostly situated in big towns, but I have never been in one place for more than three years. I have had some success as an author. My relationships with certain church officials in towns where I have preached have not always been of the best, and some of these office-bearers actually threatened me. I have been in jail three or four times for causing a breach of the peace. I am over fifty years of age, and my health is not very good. My memory is rather poor. Indeed, I have been known to forget the names of those whom I have baptised. Nevertheless, I still get quite a lot done. If you can see your way to appointing me, I shall do my best for you."

"Good heavens,' said the interim-moderator, "appoint an unhealthy, trouble-making, absent-minded jail-bird? Who on earth is the fellow?"

"Well, sir," replied the clerk, "he signs himself 'Paul'!"

That is indeed the kind of application that Paul might well have written had he applied for a congregation.

In the Hands of God pp. 102–103

O God, I know that my temper is far too quick.

I know only too well how liable I am to flare up, and to say things for which afterwards I am heartily sorry.

I know only too well that sometimes in anger I do things which in my calmer moments I would never have done.

I know that my temper upsets things at home; that it makes me difficult to work with; that it makes me lose my friends; that far too often it makes me a cause and source of trouble.

O God, help me. Help me to think before I speak. When I feel that I am going to blaze out, help me to keep quiet just for a moment or two, until I get a grip of myself again. Help me to remember that you are listening to everything I say, and seeing everything I do.

O God, control me and my temper too.

This I ask for your love's sake. Amen.

More Prayers for the Plain Man, p. 114

OURSELVES AND GOD

One Sunday, in our house, we sat listening to a television talk. We were all there, including the grand-children Jill and Karen. The speaker was talking about prayer. Jill did not seem to be paying much attention. She was, in fact, in process of getting a series of rebukes for distracting the attention of those who wanted to listen. She was bounding about in the background, climbing up the back of the couch and doing all sorts of forbidden things. After all, when you are not yet four, television talks on prayer haven't an awful lot to say to you.

The speaker had just been saying that there are certain things to remember in prayer. "God", said he, "knows far better than we do what is for our good. God is far wiser than we are." And then from the back of the sofa there came Jill's voice: "*And he's bigger, too!*" Jill had been listening after all.

God, said Jill, is a lot bigger than we are. Reinhold Neibuhr used to love to tell a story about something his daughter said when she was a little girl. One day he wanted to go for a walk, and he wanted the little girl to go with him, and she did not want to go. He painted the attractions of a walk in the open air in glowing words to persuade her, and in the end she went. When they got home, he said to her: "Well, wasn't that lovely? Aren't you glad you came?" And she answered: "I had to come. You're bigger than me!" She came because, as she saw it, she was a victim of *force majeure*.

In the Hands of God, pp. 115–116

O God, forgive me for all the things which have defeated me today.

For the times
When I knew that I ought to do something, and when I was too lazy to do it;
When I knew that I ought to help someone, and when I was too lazy to be bothered;
When I knew that I ought to keep quiet, and when I let my tongue run away with me;
When I knew that I ought to keep my temper, and when I let it flare up and blaze out;

When I knew I ought to speak, and when I remained silent
because I was too much of a coward to speak.

O God, I always start in the morning meaning to do so well,
and I seem always to finish at night after doing so badly.
Forgive me; help me; and, whatever happens, don't let
me stop trying.

This I ask for Jesus' sake. Amen.

Prayers for Young People, p. 71

THESE CHRISTFOLK!

The word *Christian* does not occur often in the New
Testament. It originated in Antioch. "In Antioch for the first
time the disciples were called Christians" (Acts 11:26). The
word is used again in the New Testament in Acts 26:28 and
in 1 Peter 4:16. The fact that the name originated in Antioch
is significant. Antioch was notorious for its ability to produce
nicknames. No one, not even the Emperor himself, was
immune from the ribald wit of the Antiochenes. Centuries
later the Emperor tried to turn the clock back and bring back
the old ways and the old gods. He himself returned to the
wearing of a beard and the Antiochenes promptly
nicknamed him The Goat! Nothing was sacred to the jesting
citizens of Antioch.

There is then little doubt that the name *Christian* was
originally a nickname. In Latin the word is *Christiani* and
in Greek *Christianoi*. The suffix *-iani* in Latin and *-ianoi* in
Greek mean *belonging to the party of*. In English we use the
suffixes *-ite* and *-er* in much the same way. So in the
Victorian days the Liberal party could be called Gladstonites;

and in the early days the Christians were mockingly called Christers.

The word Christian began as a nickname – these Christ-folk! And the Christians took a name given in mockery and made it a name than which the world knows none greater, and this name lays down the first and most important fact about the Christian – the essential thing about the Christian is his relationship to Christ. He is first and foremost a Christ-man.

The Plain Man Looks at the Apostles' Creed, pp. 265–266

O God, our Father, we thank Thee for Christmas time, and for all that it means to us.

We thank Thee that, when Jesus, Thy Son, came into this world, He came into a humble home.

We thank Thee that He had to grow up and to learn like any other boy.

We thank Thee that he did a good day's work, when He grew to manhood, as the carpenter in the village shop in Nazareth.

We thank Thee that He was tempted and tired, hungry and sad, just as we are.

We thank Thee that He was one with His brethren in all things, that He truly shared this life with its struggles and its toils, its sorrows and its joys, its trials and its temptations.

We thank Thee that He knew what it is to live in a home circle, just as we do; to earn His living, just as we do; to know friendship and to know the failure of friends, just as we know it.

We thank Thee for the service of His life; the love of His death; and the power of His Resurrection.

Grant, O God, that, when He comes to us, He may not find
that there is no room in our hearts for Him; but grant that
this Christmas day He may enter into our hearts and abide
there for evermore.

Hear this our prayer, for Thy love's sake. Amen.

The Plain Man's Book of Prayers, p. 106

THE MAN UPON MY BACK!

Jesus Christ liberates us from ourselves. Eric Linklater called
his autobiography *The Man Upon My Back*. For so many
of us our greatest handicap is our own selves; and Jesus
Christ gives us the strength and power to conquer
ourselves.

Jesus Christ liberates us from frustration. Another way of
putting that is that the tragedy of the human situation is
that we know what is right, and we cannot do it. We have
seen the dream and we cannot achieve it. We are haunted
by the impossibilities of life. Jesus Christ gives us the power
which makes the impossible possible.

Jesus Christ liberates us from fear. So many people live
in a fear-haunted life; but Jesus offers us his continual
presence in which fear must die, for with him we can face
and do anything.

Jesus Christ liberates us from sin. Through what he has
done the sin of the past is cancelled, and into life there
comes a strength in which the temptations of the future
can be conquered. Sin's penalty is removed and sin's power
is broken by the work of Christ. Redemption is the

metaphor of liberation from slavery. Jesus Christ is the great emancipator of all mankind.

The Mind of St Paul, pp. 64–65

Bless those who are ill, and who cannot sleep tonight because of their pain.
Bless those who are in hospitals, in infirmaries, and in nursing-homes; and bless the doctors and the nurses who are trying to help and to cure them.
Bless those who are sad and lonely.
Bless those who are in prison and all those who are in any kind of trouble or disgrace.
Bless those who are far away from home, amongst strange people in a strange place.
Bless all those whom I love and all those who love me.
Bless me and help me to sleep well tonight.

This I ask for Jesus' sake. Amen.

Prayers for Young People, p. 93

"I'LL MAKE ME A MAN!"

God stepped out on space,
And He looked around and said:
'I'm lonely—
I'll make me a world.'

So God made everything, and of everything he was able to say: 'That's good!'' But there was still something missing.

Then God walked around,
And God looked around
On all that He had made.
He looked at His sun,
And He looked at His moon,
And He looked at His little stars;
He looked on His world
With all its living things,
And God said: 'I'm lonely still.'
Then God sat down—
On the side of the hill where He could think;
By a deep, wide river He sat down;
With His head in His hands,
God thought and thought,
Till He thought: 'I'll make me a man!'

A child might have written that, and a child might understand that; but in it it may well be that there is the whole Christian doctrine of creation. God being love created the world and all that is in it in order to have someone to love and someone to love him. Creation is a necessity of the love of God.

The Plain Man Looks at the Apostles' Creed, pp. 55–56

Even before Christianity came into the world men have always believed that the four greatest virtues are WISDOM COURAGE, JUSTICE and SELF-CONTROL. Let us ask God to help us to have them in our lives.

O God, help me to have in my life the virtues which all men value and admire.

Give me wisdom always to know
What I ought to do;

What I ought to say;
Where I ought to go.

Give me courage,
  To do the right thing when it is difficult;
  If need be, to be laughed at for my faith;
  Never to be ashamed to show my loyalty to you.

Give me justice,
  Always to be fair in thought and word and action;
  Always to think of the rights of others as much as of my
    own;
  Never to be content when anyone is being unjustly
    treated.

Give me self-control,
  Always to have my impulses, passions and emotions
    under perfect control;
  Never to be swept into doing things for which I would
    be sorry;
  Never to do anything which would hurt others, grieve
    those who love me, or bring shame to myself.

Hear this my prayer for your love's sake. Amen.

Prayers for Young People, p. 62

"HE HAS NO HANDS BUT OUR HANDS"

The work of the Church is to bring to men the good news of the work of God in Christ. If in doing that the preacher or the missionary or the teacher suffers, then he is filling up, completing the sufferings of Christ. Christ performed his perfect work of reconciliation; the Church must tell the whole world of it; and therein the Church is the agent, the body, the complement of Christ.

Immediately a thought leaps to the mind. Does this mean that Jesus Christ is literally dependent on the Church? That is precisely and exactly what it does mean. Chrysostom, commenting on this passage, says: "See how Paul brings Christ in as needing the Church." "Such is Christ's love for the Church that he, as it were, regards himself as incomplete, unless he has the Church united to him as a body."

However startling the dependence of Christ on men may appear to be, it is demonstrably true. There is a sense in which we can speak of the divine helplessness. If Jesus Christ wants a child taught, nothing will teach that child, unless some man or woman is prepared to do so. If Jesus Christ wants a land evangelized, the purpose of Christ is frustrated, unless men and women are prepared to go out into the world and preach the gospel. Jesus Christ is not now here in the body, although he is powerfully here in the Spirit and in his risen presence; if, therefore, he wants anything done in this world he has to get a man or a woman to do it for him. That is the real sense in which the Church is the body of Christ. To say that the Church is the body of Christ is to say that we must be hands through which he can work, we must be voices through which he can speak, we must be feet with which he can travel, we must be the agents he can send and the instruments he can use.

> He has no hands but our hands
>   To do his work today,
> He has no feet but our feet
>   To lead men in his way.
> He has no voice but our voice
>   To tell men how he died,

He has no help but our help
To lead men to his side.

The Plain Man Looks at the Apostles' Creed, pp. 288–289

O God, you know me, and you know that I don't want to go out at all today.

I am tired before I start. There are people I don't want to meet; there are jobs I don't want to do. There are tasks which I will have to do, and I am not nearly as well prepared for them as I ought to be.

I would much rather stay at home, or run away from it all. But I can't do that, and I know I can't do that. I know quite well life has got to go on, no matter how I feel about it.

Lord Jesus, come with me, and help me to feel you beside me all day, so that I will not only get grimly through today, but that I may know the joy of living with you.

This I ask for you love's sake. Amen.

More Prayers for the Plain Man, p. 64

JESUS, OUR SUBSTITUTE

In the most literal sense Jesus Christ bore the divine punishment that should have fallen on us, and gathered to himself the divine wrath which should have been directed against us.

There is a certain moving magnificence in this thought.

This is the kind of action which moves the hearts of men. David Smith quotes a human example of this spirit: Fergus MacIvor, as Scott tells in *Waverley*, was sentenced to death at Carlisle for his part in the 1745 rebellion. In the court was one of his clansmen, Evan Maccombich. Evan addressed the judge: " 'I was only ganging to say, my lord, that if your excellent honour and the honourable court would let Vich Ian Vohr go free just this once, and let him gae back to France, and no' to trouble King George's government again, that ony six o' the very best of his clan will be willing to be judgified in his stead; and if you'll just let me gae down to Glennaquoich, I'll fetch them up to ye mysell, to head or hang, and you may begin wi' me the very first man.' There was a titter in the court at this extraordinary offer, but the judge silenced it. Evan went on: 'If the Saxon gentlemen are laughing because a poor man, such as me, thinks my life, or the life of six of my degree, is worth that of Vich Ian Vohr, it's like enough they may be very right; but if they laugh because they think I would not keep my word and come back to redeem him, I can tell them they ken neither the heart of a Hielandman nor the honour of a gentleman.' " And then Scott ends the story: "There was no further inclination to laugh among the audience, and a dead silence ensued."

There is nothing moves the heart like the picture of a man ready to lay down his life for his friend, the picture of a man with such a love that he will willingly bear what someone else should have borne. And that is the picture of Jesus our substitute.

The Plain Man Looks at the Apostles' Creed, pp. 110–111

O God, take control of me all through today.
Control my tongue
  so that I may speak
    No angry word;
    No cruel word;
    No untrue word;
    No ugly word.
Control my thoughts,
  so that I may think
    No impure thoughts;
    No bitter, envious, or jealous thoughts;
    No selfish thoughts.
Control my actions,
  so that all through today
    My work may be my best;
    I may never be too busy to lend a hand to those who need it;
    I may do nothing of which afterwards I would be ashamed.

All this I ask for Jesus' sake. Amen.

Prayers for Young People, p. 34

THE MAN WITH THE GOLDEN KEY

There is a sense in which education has broken down. There are areas with schools out of which a child will come never having written one single line in answer to any question, unable to put a paragraph together on paper. There are levels of education out of which the child will come with no reading desire other than the strip cartoon or the comic.

When G. K. Chesterton was a child he had a cardboard toy theatre with cut-out characters. One of the characters was a man with a golden key; he never could remember what character that man with the golden key represented; but that character was always identified in his mind with his father, whom he saw as a man with a golden key who unlocked all sorts of doors leading to all sorts of wonderful things. The dream of education is that education should be a golden key to unlock the doors, not simply to the skills which are necessary to make a living, but to the things of the human spirit, of art, of music, of drama, by which men and women will find life.

Ethics in a Permissive Society, p. 103

O God, help me to be cheerful all through today,
  Whatever I have to do, help me to do it with a smile.
O God, help me to be diligent all through today,
  Whatever I have to do, help me to do my best.
O God, help me to be kind all through today,
  Whatever I have to do, help me not to be too busy to help
    someone else.
O God, help me to be brave all through today,
  Whatever I have to do, help me to face it and not to dodge
    it.
O God, help me to be reverent all through today,
  Whatever I have to do, help me to remember that you see
    me, and help me to make every word fit for you to hear,
    and every bit of work fit to offer to you.

This I ask for your love's sake. Amen.

Prayers for Young People, p. 66

THE FLOCK OF GOD

In any terms the picture of the Church as the flock of God is a lovely picture, but it is even lovelier when it is set against its Palestinian background. The pasture land of Judaea is no more than a narrow ridge like the backbone of the country. There were no walled fields, and the pasture land either plunged in cliffs down to the Dead Sea or fell away in infertile valleys through the Shephelah to the Mediterranean coast. The wandering sheep would certainly perish, and even on the pasture land itself grass was sparse and wells and springs were few and far between. The result of this was that in Palestine a flock was never to be seen without its shepherd. Day and night the shepherd was on constant guard; without his constant and unsleeping care the sheep would certainly starve or wander to disaster.

The picture of the Church as the flock of God underlines the twin facts of God's unceasing care for his Church, and of the Church's complete dependence upon God. In the picture of the flock we see at one and the same time the love of God and the need of man.

The Plain Man Looks at the Apostles' Creed, p. 271

Eternal and everblessed God, we remember this day the unseen cloud of witnesses who compass us about. We remember the blessed dead who do rest from their labours, and whose works do follow them. And we give Thee thanks for all of them.

For parents who gave us life; who tended and cared for us in years when we were helpless to help ourselves; who toiled and sacrificed to give to us our chance in

life; at whose knees we learned to pray, and from whose lips we first heard the name of Jesus:
> We give Thee thanks, O God.

For teachers who taught us;
For ministers of Thy gospel who instructed us in Thy truth and in Thy faith;
For all those who have been an example to us of what life should be;
For those whose influence on us will never cease, and whose names will never depart from our memory;
> We give Thee thanks, O God.

For the saints, the prophets and the martyrs;
For those who lived and died for the faith;
And, above all else, for Jesus, the captain of our salvation and the author and finisher of our faith:
> We give Thee thanks, O God.

Grant unto us in our day and generation to walk worthily of the heritage into which we have entered: through Jesus Christ our Lord. Amen.

The Plain Man's Book of Prayers, p. 104

MISSING THE TARGET

As soon as we have disobeyed the voice of God, and sinned, another element enters into the situation, through sin we *come short* of the glory of God (Romans 3:23). What does that mean? When we go back to the old story of creation we find that God made man in his own image, and his own likeness (Genesis 1:26). That is to say God made man to bear his own image, and therefore to reflect his own glory. Sin therefore is what keeps a man from being what he was meant to be and what he was created to be. Here we come at the basic meaning of *hamartia*. *Hamartia* was not originally an ethical word at all. It was, in fact, a word from shooting; and it meant *a missing of the target*. Sin is the failure to hit the target; sin is the failure to be what we were meant to be; sin is falling below one's own possibilities. The moment a man begins to disobey he begins to lose the image of God, and therefore falls short of what he was meant to be. Here is the very foundation in practice of the universality of sin. To fail to do one's best as workman, to fail to be as good a father, mother, son, daughter as one might have been, to fail to use and to develop the gifts of hand and eye and mind and brain that God has given us, in any way to fall short of the best that we could be is a sin. Disobedience to God means failure in life; and failure to hit the target is sin.

The Mind of St Paul, p. 141

O God, help me to conquer the things which would keep me from being what I can be, and what I ought to be:

The inattention which makes me let things go in at one ear and out at the other;

The careless workmanship which does not put its best into every job;

The self-will which makes me resent and refuse guidance, and makes me take my own way – so often to trouble;

The laziness which makes me do nothing when all kinds of things are needing to be done;

The ingratitude which hurts those who have been kind to me;

115

The cowardice which makes me go with the crowd
because I am afraid to stand alone;
The disloyalty which makes me let down my friends and
disappoint those who love me—

Preserve me from all these things, O God. Strengthen me
where I am weak; correct me where I am wrong; cleanse
and purify me from all the faults which spoil my life;
through Jesus Christ my Lord. Amen.

More Prayers for Young People, p. 32

IF WE LOVE SOMEONE, THEN SURELY WE CANNOT HELP PRAYING FOR THEM

The greatest thing that we can do for any man is to pray
for him. Alexander Whyte told a story of a servant girl who
was a member of his congregation. When she came asking
to become a member, he asked her what she could do for
her church and for the work of Jesus Christ. It was in the
old days when the work of a domestic servant lasted all
day and half the night. "I haven't much time to do things,"
the girl said, "but at night, when I go to bed, I take the
morning newspaper with me." "Yes," said Whyte,
wondering what could possibly be coming next. "And,"
the girl went on, "I read the birth notices, and I pray for
the little babies who have just come into the world. I read
the marriage notices, and I pray that God will give these
people happiness. I read the death notices, and I pray that
God will comfort those who are sad." No one in this world
will ever know what blessing to unknown people came

from an attic bedroom from one who prayed. If we love someone, then surely we cannot help praying for them.

More Prayers for the Plain Man, pp. 17–18

Save me from being altogether selfish in my prayers, and help me to remember others who are in trouble.

The sick and those who must lie in bed throughout the sunlit hours, especially young folk laid aside too soon in the morning of their day;

Those who are sad and sorry because someone they loved has died;

Those who are disappointed because something they wanted very much has passed them by;

The discontented, those who live with a chip on their shoulder, who are their own worst enemies;

Those who have done something wrong and who are in disgrace, that they may redeem themselves;

Those who are underrated and undervalued, and who have never been appreciated as they ought to have been;

Those who have been passed over for some office they had expected to receive;

All those in pain, in sorrow, in misfortune, in disgrace:

Bless all such. For your love's sake I ask it. Amen.

More Prayers for Young People, p. 64

PEACE OF HEART

The history of the Church of England has an outstanding example of this principle in action. Thomas Cranmer was Archbishop of Canterbury; he had leanings towards Protestantism and he was closely affiliated to the Protestants. When Mary came to the throne, and she began her persecuting career in her attempt to obliterate Protestantism, Cranmer was arrested. Thereupon to save his life he signed no fewer than six recantations of all his connection with Protestantism. His recantations did not in the end succeed in saving his life; but when the time came to die, Cranmer found a new courage. In St Mary's Church in Oxford he was brought forward to repeat his recantations. Instead of doing so he ended his address to the deeply moved congregation: "Now I come to the great thing that troubleth my conscience more than any other thing I said or did in my life, and that is the setting abroad of writings contrary to the truth, which here I now renounce and refuse as things written by my hand contrary to the truth I thought in my heart, and written for fear of death to save my life, if it might be. And forasmuch as my hand offended in writing contrary to my heart, my hand, therefore, shall be the first punished; for, if I come to the fire, it shall be the first burned." And, when he did come to the stake, he held out his hand and put it into the flames saying: "This was the hand that wrote it, therefore, it shall suffer first punishment." And, holding it steadily in the flames, "he never stirred nor cried till life was gone". For Cranmer the joy of martyrdom was far greater than the joy of escape. To evade persecution may be to escape trouble for the moment, but in the end it is to beget that self-contempt which makes life intolerable. To face persecution may bring the agony of the moment,

but in the end it is the way to satisfaction and to peace
of heart.

The Plain Man Looks at the Beatitudes, pp. 117–118

O God,
I can no longer pretend to myself
    that everything will be all right
    if I just leave things alone.
I can no longer avoid the fact
    that there is something wrong.
Go with me when I go to my doctor today,
    and give me courage to face the truth about myself.
Make me quite sure that, whatever the verdict,
    I can face it with you.

Let me remember the promise of God:
When you pass through the waters I will be with you.
                                            Isaiah 43:2

My times are in thy hand:
Why should I doubt or fear?
My Father's hand will never cause
His child a needless tear.

Prayers for Help and Healing, p. 21

ABRAHAM

Paul knew quite well that very few people can grasp abstract
truths and abstract ideas; he was a wise teacher and he knew
that nearly everyone thinks in pictures and that, if we

want to present a person with an idea, that idea must become vivid and concrete and dramatic in a picture. So Paul turns the word faith into flesh; he turns the idea of faith into a person, and that person is Abraham. It is in Romans 4 and Galatians 3 that this idea is most fully worked out. Abraham was justified; that is to say, Abraham was in a right relationship with God. How did Abraham arrive at that right relationship? It was certainly not by keeping the Law, for the simple reason that the Law was not given until four hundred years after Abraham was dead. It was certainly not through circumcision because Abraham was in his right relationship with God years before he was circumcised. The promise and the blessing and the right relationship came to Abraham quite independently of the Law and of circumcision.

Wherein then lay Abraham's faith? Put at its very briefest – Abraham went out now knowing whither he went. Put in another way – Abraham took God absolutely and completely at his word. Let us put it in still another way – Abraham's faith was compounded of perfect trust and absolute obedience. Abraham took God at his word when God promised and when God commanded, and that is faith.

The Mind of St Paul, p. 111

Forgive me, O God,
For the time I have wasted today;
For the people I have hurt today;
For the tasks I have shirked today.

Help me
Not to be discouraged when things are difficult;
Not to be content with second bests;
To do better tomorrow than I have done today.

And help me always to remember that Jesus is with me and
that I am not trying all alone.

This I ask for Jesus' sake. Amen.

Prayers for Young People, p. 63

OUR FAITH

There is a wondeerful unwritten saying of Jesus, a saying
which is not in any of the Gospels, but which is surely his:
Jesus said: *Wherever they may be they are not without God; and
where there is one alone, even then I am with him. Raise the stone
and there you will find me; cleave the wood and I am there.* Where
the mason works at the stone and where the carpenter
works at the wood, Jesus Christ is there. We have only to
compare that saying with the saying of a man who did not
know Jesus Christ. The ancient preacher wrote: "Who hews
stones shall be hurt by them; who cleaves wood is
endangered by it" (Ecclesiastes 10:9). For the Christless
man, work was a penance and a peril; for the man who
knows the risen Christ, work is a sharing of the presence
of the risen Lord. "Work", as Jeremias puts it, "is a blessing,
because it is hallowed by the presence of Jesus."

> And warm, sweet, tender, even yet
> A present help is He;
> And faith has still its Olivet,
> And love its Galilee.

With the Easter faith, with the presence of the risen Lord,
life becomes a glory.
  It is the Easter faith, the faith in the risen and living Lord,

121

which makes us able to meet death. It is the Easter faith that we have a Friend and a Companion who lived and who died and who is alive for evermore, who is the Conqueror of death. The presence which is with us in life is with us in death and beyond.

A writer tells how his father died. His father was old and ill. One morning the writer tells how he went up to his father's bedroom to waken him. The old man said: ''Pull up the blinds so that I can see the morning light.'' The son pulled up the blind, and even as the light entered the room, the old man sank back on his pillows dead. Death was the coming of the morning light.

It is time that we were thinking of Easter. The Easter faith should be in our thoughts not simply at a certain season of the Christian year; it ought to be the faith in which Christians daily live, and in which they die, only to live again.

In the Hands of God, pp. 106–107

After entering hospital

O God,
Everything is new and strange and rather frightening.
Half the time I don't know what is going on.
Help me
    to be serene and calm and relaxed.
Keep me cheerful,
    and help me to be a comrade
    to those who are feeling
    just as strange and just as afraid as I am.
Help me
    not to grumble or complain.
Help me
    to be grateful for all that is done for me.

Help me
  to make the work of those who are looking after me as
  easy as I can.
Help me
  to forget my own troubles
  in doing something to help and cheer
  those who are worse off than I am.

Help me to be as sure of God as the Psalmist was when he
said:

God is our refuge and strength,
a very present help in trouble.   *Psalm 46:1*

  Hold thou my hands!
In grief and joy, in hope and fear,
Lord, let me feel that thou art near;
  Hold thou my hands!

Prayers for Help and Healing, p. 23